IN A HEROIC AGE, on the vast plains of North India, a timeless spiritual classic was born – the message of Sri Krishna to Prince Arjuna, on the brink of a war he doesn't want to fight.

Arjuna's struggle in the Bhagavad Gita is acutely modern. He has lost his way on the battlefield of life and turns to find the path again by asking direct, uncompromising questions of his spiritual guide, Sri Krishna, the Lord himself.

Krishna replies in 700 verses of sublime instruction on living and dying, loving and working, and the nature of the soul.

Easwaran shows the Gita's relevance to us today as we strive, like Arjuna, to do what is right.

THE BHAGAVAD GITA

On this path effort never goes to waste,
and there is no failure. Even a little effort
toward spiritual awareness will protect you
from the greatest fear. (2:40)

CLASSICS OF

INDIAN SPIRITUALITY

❏❖

The Bhagavad Gita

The Dhammapada

The Upanishads

The Bhagavad Gita

Introduced &

Translated by

EKNATH
EASWARAN

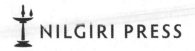 NILGIRI PRESS

Second edition, first printing:
paperback 2007   hardcover 2019
20 19 18 17 16 15 14   10 9 8 7 6 5 4 3
Printed in Canada on recycled paper

ISBN: 978-1-58638-019-9 *(paperback)*
ISBN: 978-1-58638-130-1 *(hardcover)*
ISBN: 978-1-58638-023-6 *(ebook)*
ISBN: 978-1-58638-747-1 *(audiobook)*

Library of Congress Control Number: 2006934966

Publisher's Cataloging-In-Publication Data
(Prepared by The Donohue Group, Inc.)

Bhagavadgītā. English.
  The Bhagavad Gita / introduced & translated by Eknath Easwaran. -- 2nd ed.
  p. ; cm.   -- (Classics of Indian spirituality)
  Includes index.
  ISBN-13 : 978-1-58638-019-9
  ISBN-10 : 1-58638-019-2
I. Easwaran, Eknath. II. Title.
BL1138.62 .E5 2007
294.5/924   2006934966

Nilgiri Press is the publishing division of the Blue Mountain
Center of Meditation, a nonprofit organization founded by
Eknath Easwaran in 1961.
www.bmcm.org | info@bmcm.org
The Blue Mountain Center of Meditation
Box 256, Tomales, California 94971-0256 USA
Telephone: +1 707 878 2369 | 800 475 2369

❏ *Table of Contents*

Foreword 7

Introduction 13

1 *The War Within 71*

2 *Self-Realization 83*

3 *Selfless Service 99*

4 *Wisdom in Action 111*

5 *Renounce & Rejoice 123*

6 *The Practice of Meditation 133*

7 *Wisdom from Realization 147*

8 *The Eternal Godhead 157*

9 *The Royal Path 169*

10 *Divine Splendor 179*

11 *The Cosmic Vision 191*

12 *The Way of Love* 203

13 *The Field & the Knower* 211

14 *The Forces of Evolution* 221

15 *The Supreme Self* 229

16 *Two Paths* 235

17 *The Power of Faith* 243

18 *Freedom & Renunciation* 251

Notes 267

Glossary 277

Index 289

❏ *The Classics of Indian Spirituality*

IMAGINE A VAST hall in Anglo-Saxon England, not long after the passing of King Arthur. It is the dead of winter and a fierce snowstorm rages outside, but a great fire fills the space within the hall with warmth and light. Now and then, a sparrow darts in for refuge from the weather. It appears as if from nowhere, flits about joyfully in the light, and then disappears again, and where it comes from and where it goes next in that stormy darkness, we do not know.

Our lives are like that, suggests an old story in Bede's medieval history of England. We spend our days in the familiar world of our five senses, but what lies beyond that, if anything, we have no idea. Those sparrows are hints of something more outside – a vast world, perhaps, waiting to be explored. But most of us are happy to stay where we are. We may even be a bit afraid to venture into the unknown. What would be the point, we ask. Why should we leave the world we know?

Yet there are always a few who are not content to spend their lives indoors. Simply knowing there is something unknown beyond their reach makes them acutely restless. They have to see what lies outside – if only, as George Mallory said of Everest, "because it's there."

This is true of adventurers of every kind, but especially of those who seek to explore not mountains or jungles but consciousness itself: whose real drive, we might say, is not so much to know the unknown as to know the knower. Such men and women can be found in every age and every culture. While the rest of us stay put, they quietly slip out to see what lies beyond.

Then, so far as we can tell, they disappear. We have no idea where they have gone; we can't even imagine. But every now and then, like friends who have run off to some exotic land, they send back reports: breathless messages describing fantastic adventures, rambling letters about a world beyond ordinary experience, urgent telegrams begging us to come and see. "Look at this view! Isn't it breathtaking? Wish you could see this. Wish you were here."

The works in this set of translations – the Upanishads, the Bhagavad Gita, and the Dhammapada – are among the earliest and most universal of messages like these, sent to inform us that there is more to life than the everyday experience of our senses. The Upanishads are the oldest, so varied that we feel some unknown collectors must have tossed into a jumble all the photos, postcards, and letters from this world that they could find, without any regard for source or circumstance.

Thrown together like this, they form a kind of ecstatic slide-show – snapshots of towering peaks of consciousness taken at various times by different observers and dispatched with just the barest kind of explanation. But those who have traveled those heights will recognize the views: "Oh, yes, that's Everest from the northwest – must be late spring. And here we're south, in the full snows of winter."

The Dhammapada, too, is a collection – traditionally, sayings of the Buddha, one of the very greatest of these explorers of consciousness. In this case the messages have been sorted, but not by a scheme that makes sense to us today. Instead of being grouped by theme or topic, they are gathered according to some dominant characteristic like a symbol or metaphor – flowers, birds, a river, the sky – that makes them easy to commit to memory. If the Upanishads are like slides, the Dhammapada seems more like a field guide. This is lore picked up by someone who knows every step of the way through these strange lands. He can't take us there, he explains, but he can show us the way: tell us what to look for, warn about missteps, advise us about detours, tell us what to avoid. Most important, he urges us that it is our destiny as human beings to make this journey ourselves. Everything else is secondary.

And the third of these classics, the Bhagavad Gita, gives us a map and guidebook. It gives a systematic overview of the territory, shows various approaches to the summit with their benefits and pitfalls, offers recommendations, tells us what to pack and what to leave behind. More than either of the others, it gives the sense of a personal guide. It asks and answers the questions that you or I might ask – questions not about philosophy or mysticism, but about how to live effectively in a world of challenge and change. Of these three, it is the Gita that has been my own personal guidebook, just as it was Mahatma Gandhi's.

These three texts are very personal records of a landscape that is both real and universal. Their voices, passionately human, speak directly to you and me. They describe the topography of consciousness itself, which belongs as much to us today as to these largely anonymous seers thousands of years ago. If the landscape seems dark in the light of sense perception, they tell us, it has an illumination of its own, and once our eyes adjust we can see in what Western mystics call this "divine dark" and verify their descriptions for ourselves.

And this world, they insist, is where we belong. This wider field of consciousness is our native land. We are not cabin-dwellers, born to a life cramped and confined; we are meant to explore, to seek, to push the limits of our potential as human beings. The world of the senses is just a base camp: we are meant to be as much at home in consciousness as in the world of physical reality.

This is a message that thrills men and women in every age and culture. It is for such kindred spirits that these texts were originally composed, and it is for them in our own time that

I undertook these translations, in the conviction that they deserve an audience today as much as ever. If these books speak to even a handful of such readers, they will have served their purpose.

❚: *The Bhagavad Gita*

MANY YEARS AGO, when I was still a graduate student, I traveled by train from central India to Simla, then the summer seat of the British government in India. We had not been long out of Delhi when suddenly a chattering of voices disturbed my reverie. I asked the man next to me if something had happened. "Kurukshetra!" he replied. "The next stop is Kurukshetra!"

I could understand the excitement. Kurukshetra, "the field of the Kurus," is the setting for the climactic battle of the *Mahabharata,* the vastest epic in any world literature, on which virtually every Hindu child in India is raised. Its characters, removed in time by some three thousand years, are as familiar to us as our relatives. The temper of the story is utterly contemporary; I can imagine it unfolding in the nuclear age as easily as in the dawn of Indian history. The *Mahabharata* is literature at its greatest – in fact, it has been called a literature in itself, comparable in its breadth and depth and characterization to the whole of Greek literature or Shakespeare. But what makes it unique is that embedded in this literary masterpiece is one of the finest mystical documents the world has seen: the Bhagavad Gita.

I must have heard the Gita recited thousands of times when I was growing up, but I don't suppose it had any special significance for me then. Not until I went to college and met Mahatma Gandhi did I begin to understand why nothing in the long, rich stretch of Indian culture has had a wider appeal, not only within India but outside as well. Today, after more than thirty years of devoted study, I would not hesitate to call it India's most important gift to the world. The Gita has been translated into every major language and perhaps a hundred times into English alone; commentaries on it are said to be more numerous than on any other scripture. Like the Sermon on the Mount, it has an immediacy that sweeps away time, place, and circumstance. Addressed to everyone, of whatever background or status, the Gita distills the loftiest truths of India's ancient wisdom into simple, memorable poetry that haunts the mind and informs the affairs of everyday life.

Everyone in our car got down from the train to wander for a few minutes on the now peaceful field. Thousands of years ago this was Armageddon. The air rang with the conch-horns and shouts of battle for eighteen days. Great phalanxes shaped like eagles and fish and the crescent moon surged back and forth in search of victory, until in the end almost every warrior in the land lay slain.

"Imagine!" my companion said to me in awe. "Bhishma and Drona commanded their armies here. Arjuna rode here, with Sri Krishna himself as his charioteer. Where you're standing now – who knows? – Arjuna might have sat, his bow and arrows on the ground, while Krishna gave him the words of the Bhagavad Gita."

The thought was thrilling. I felt the way Schliemann must have when he finally reached that desolate bluff of western Turkey and knew he was standing "on the ringing plains of windy Troy," walking the same ground as Achilles, Odysseus, Hector, and Helen. Yet at the same time, I felt I knew the setting of the Gita much more intimately than I could ever know this peaceful field. The battlefield is a perfect backdrop, but the Gita's subject is the war within, the struggle for self-mastery that every human being must wage if he or she is to emerge from life victorious.

THE GITA AND ITS SETTING

Historians surmise that like the *Iliad*, the *Mahabharata* might well be based on actual events, culminating in a war that took place somewhere around 1000 B.C. – close, that is, to the very dawn of recorded Indian history. This guess has recently been supported by excavations at the ancient city of Dvaraka, which, according to the *Mahabharata,* was destroyed and submerged in the sea after the departure of its divine ruler, Krishna. Only five hundred years or so before this, by generally accepted guess, Aryan tribes originally from the area between the Caspian Sea and the Hindu Kush mountains had migrated into the Indian subcontinent, bringing the prototype of the Sanskrit language and countless elements of belief and culture that have been part of the Hindu tradition ever since. The oldest part of the most ancient of Hindu scriptures, the Rig Veda, dates from this period – about 1500 B.C., if not earlier.

Yet the wellspring of Indian religious faith, I believe, can be traced to a much earlier epoch. When the Aryans entered the Indian subcontinent through the mountains of the Hindu Kush, they encountered a civilization on the banks of the Indus river that archeologists date back as far as 3000 B.C. Roughly contemporaneous with the pyramid-builders on the Nile, these Indus-dwellers achieved a comparable level of technology. They had metalworkers skilled in sheet-making, riveting, and casting of copper and bronze, crafts and industries with standardized methods of production, land and sea trade with cultures as far away as Mesopotamia, and well-planned cities with water supply and public sanitation systems unequaled until the Romans. Evidence suggests that they may have used a decimal system of measurement. But most remarkable, images of Shiva as Yogeshvara, the Lord of Yoga, suggest that meditation was practiced in a civilization which flourished a millennium before the Vedas were committed to an oral tradition.

If this is so, it would imply that the same systematic attitude the Indus Valley dwellers applied to their technology was applied also to study of the mind. This was *brahmavidya*, the "supreme science" – supreme because where other sciences studied the external world, brahmavidya sought knowledge of an underlying reality which would inform all other studies and activities.

Whatever its origins, in the early part of the first millennium B.C. we find clearly stated both the methods and the discoveries of brahmavidya. With this introspective tool the inspired *rishis* (literally "seers") of ancient India analyzed their awareness of human experience to see if there was anything in it that was absolute. Their findings can be summarized in three statements which Aldous Huxley, following Leibnitz, has called the Perennial Philosophy because they appear in every age and civilization: (1) there is an infinite, changeless reality beneath the world of change; (2) this same reality lies at the core of every human personality; (3) the purpose of life is to discover this reality experientially: that is, to realize God while here on earth. These principles and the interior experiments for realizing them were taught systematically in "forest academies" or ashrams – a tradition which continues unbroken after some three thousand years.

The discoveries of brahmavidya were systematically committed to memory (and eventually to writing) in the Upanishads, visionary documents that are the earliest and purest statement of the Perennial Philosophy. How many of these precious records once existed no one knows; a dozen that date from Vedic times have survived as part of the Hindu canon of authority, the four Vedas. All have one unmistakable hallmark: the vivid stamp of personal mystical experience. These are records of direct encounter with the divine. Tradition calls them *shruti*: literally "heard," as opposed to learned; they are their own authority. By convention, only the Vedas (including their Upanishads) are considered shruti, based on direct knowledge of God.

According to this definition, all other Indian scriptures – including the Gita – are secondary, dependent on the higher authority of the Vedas. However, this is a conventional distinction and one that might disguise the nature of the documents it classifies. In the literal sense the Gita too is shruti, owing its authority not to other scriptures but to the fact that it set down the direct mystical experience of a single author. Shankara, a towering mystic of the ninth century A.D. whose word carries the authority of Augustine, Eckhart, and Aquinas all in one, must have felt this, for in selecting the minimum sources of Hinduism he passed over almost a hundred Upanishads of Vedic authority to choose ten central Upanishads and the Bhagavad Gita.

The Gita, I would argue, is not an integral part of the *Mahabharata*. It is essentially an Upanishad, and my conjecture is that it was set down by an inspired seer (traditionally Vyasa) and inserted into the epic at the appropriate place. Other elements were added in this way to the *Mahabharata*, and to other popular secondary scriptures; it is an effective way of preserving new material in an oral tradition. There is also traditional weight behind this idea, for as far back as anyone can trace, each chapter of the Gita has ended with the same formula: "In the Bhagavad-Gita Upanishad, the text on the supreme science [*brahmavidya*] of yoga, this is the chapter entitled..."

Finally, by way of further support, we can observe that except for its first chapter, which sets the stage, the Gita not only does not develop the action of the *Mahabharata* but is rather at odds with it. Battle lines are drawn – the climax of decades of dissension – and on the eve of combat, Prince Arjuna loses his nerve and asks his charioteer, Krishna, what to do. Then what? Krishna – no ordinary charioteer, but an incarnation of God – enters into some seven hundred verses of sublime instruction on the nature of the soul and its relation to God, the levels of consciousness and reality, the makeup of the phenomenal world, and so on, culminating in a stupendous mystical experience in which he reveals himself to Arjuna as the transcendent Lord of life and death. He counsels Arjuna to be compassionate to friend and enemy alike, to see himself in every person, to suffer others' sorrows as his own. Then the Gita is over, the narration picks up again, and battle is joined – a terrible, desperate slaughter compromising everyone's honor, by the end of which Arjuna's side emerges victorious. But almost every man of fighting age on both sides has been slain. Only great genius would have placed the Gita in such a dramatic setting, but it stands out from the rest as a timeless, practical manual for daily living.

To those who take this dramatic setting as part of the spiritual instruction and get entangled in the question of the Gita justifying war, Gandhi had a practical answer: just base your life on the Gita sincerely and systematically and see if you find killing or even hurting others compatible with its teachings. (He makes the same point of the Sermon on the Mount.) The very heart of the Gita's message is to see the Lord in every creature and act accordingly, and the scripture is full of verses to spell out what this means:

I am ever present to those who have realized me in every creature. Seeing all life as my manifestation, they are never separated from me. They worship me in the hearts of all, and all their actions proceed from me. Wherever they may live, they abide in me. (6:30–31)

When a person responds to the joys and sorrows of others as if they were his own, he has attained the highest state of spiritual union. (6:32)

That one I love who is incapable of ill will, who is friendly and compassionate. (12:13)

They alone see truly who see the Lord the same in every

creature, who see the deathless in the hearts of all that
die. Seeing the same Lord everywhere, they do not harm
themselves or others. Thus they attain the supreme goal.
(13:27–28)

Scholars can debate the point forever, but when the Gita
is practiced, I think, it becomes clear that the struggle the
Gita is concerned with is the struggle for self-mastery. It was
Vyasa's genius to take the whole great *Mahabharata* epic and
see it as metaphor for the perennial war between the forces of
light and the forces of darkness in every human heart. Arjuna
and Krishna are then no longer merely characters in a literary masterpiece. Arjuna becomes Everyman, asking the Lord
himself, Sri Krishna, the perennial questions about life and
death – not as a philosopher, but as the quintessential man of
action. Thus read, the Gita is not an external dialogue but an
internal one: between the ordinary human personality, full
of questions about the meaning of life, and our deepest Self,
which is divine.

There is, in fact, no other way to read the Gita and grasp it
as spiritual instruction. If I could offer only one key to understanding this divine dialogue, it would be to remember that it
takes place in the depths of consciousness and that Krishna
is not some external being, human or superhuman, but the
spark of divinity that lies at the core of the human personality.
This is not literary or philosophical conjecture; Krishna says

as much to Arjuna over and over: "I am the Self in the heart of every creature, Arjuna, and the beginning, middle, and end of their existence" (10:20).

In such statements the Gita distills the essence of the Upanishads, not piecemeal but comprehensively, offering their lofty insights as a manual not of philosophy but of everyday human activity – a handbook of the Perennial Philosophy unique in world history.

THE UPANISHADIC BACKGROUND

The Gita, naturally enough, takes for granted that its audience is familiar with the basic ideas of Hindu religious thought, almost all of which can be found in the Upanishads. It also uses some technical vocabulary from yoga psychology. All this needs to be explained in contemporary terms if the modern reader is to grasp what is essential and timeless in the Gita's message and not get bogged down in strange terminology.

First, however, the non-Hindu faces a third obstacle: the multiplicity of names used for aspects of God. From the earliest times, Hinduism has proclaimed one God while accommodating worship of him (or her, for to millions God is the Divine Mother) in many different names. "Truth is one," says a famous verse of the Rig Veda; "people call it by various names." Monastic devotees might find that Shiva embodies the austere detachment they seek; devotees who want to live "in the world," partaking of its innocent pleasures but devoted to service of their fellow creatures, might find in Krishna the perfect incarnation of their ideals. In every case, this clothing of the Infinite in human form serves to focus a devotee's love and to provide an inspiring ideal. But whatever form is worshipped, it is only an aspect of the same one God.

In the Gita – in fact, virtually everywhere in Hindu myth and scripture – we also encounter "the gods" in the plural. These are the *devas,* deities which seem to have come in with the Aryans and which have recognizable counterparts in other Aryan-influenced cultures: Indra, god of war and storm; Varuna, god of waters and a moral overseer; Agni, god of fire, the Hermes-like intermediary between heaven and earth; and so on. The Gita refers to the devas as being worshipped by those who want to propitiate natural and supernatural powers, in much the same way that ancestors were worshipped. In modern terms, they can best be understood as personifying the forces of nature.

This question out of the way, we can proceed to the Upanishadic background the Gita assumes.

Atman and Brahman

The Upanishads are not systematic philosophy; they are more like ecstatic slide shows of mystical experience – vivid, disjointed, stamped with the power of direct personal encounter with the divine. If they seem to embrace contradictions, that is because they do not try to smooth over the seams of these experiences. They simply set down what the rishis saw, viewing the ultimate reality from different levels of spiritual awareness, like snapshots of the same object from different angles: now seeing God as utterly transcendent, for example, now seeing God as immanent as well. These differences are not important, and the Upanishads agree on their central ideas: *Brahman,* the Godhead; *Atman,* the divine core of personality; *dharma,* the law that expresses and maintains the unity of creation; *karma,* the web of cause and effect; *samsara,* the cycle of birth and death; *moksha,* the spiritual liberation that is life's supreme goal.

Even while ancient India was making breakthroughs in the natural sciences and mathematics, the sages of the Upanishads were turning inward to analyze the data that nature presents to the mind. Penetrating below the senses, they found not a world of solid, separate objects but a ceaseless process of change – matter coming together, dissolving, and coming together again in a different form. Below this flux of things with "name and form," however, they found something changeless: an infinite, indivisible reality in which the transient data of the world cohere. They called this reality Brahman: the Godhead, the divine ground of existence.

This analysis of the phenomenal world tallies well enough with contemporary physics. A physicist would remind us that the things we see "out there" are not ultimately separate from each other and from us; we perceive them as separate because of the limitations of our senses. If our eyes were sensitive to a much finer spectrum, we might see the world as a continuous field of matter and energy. Nothing in this picture resembles a solid object in our usual sense of the word. "The external world of physics," wrote Sir Arthur Eddington, "has thus become a world of shadows. In removing our illusions we remove the substance, for indeed we have seen that substance is one of the greatest of our illusions." Like the physicists, these ancient sages were seeking an invariant. They found it in Brahman.

In examining our knowledge of ourselves, the sages made a similar discovery. Instead of a single coherent personality, they found layer on layer of components – senses, emotions, will, intellect, ego – each in flux. At different times and in different company, the same person seems to have different personalities. Moods shift and flicker, even in those who are emotionally stable; desires and opinions change with time. Change is the nature of the mind. The sages observed this flow of thoughts and sensations and asked, "Then where am I?" The parts do not add up to a whole; they just flow by. Like physical phenomena, the mind is a field of forces, no more the seat of intelligence than radiation or gravity is. Just as the world dissolves into a sea of energy, the mind dissolves into a river of impressions and thoughts, a flow of fragmentary data that do not hold together.

Western philosophers have reasoned their way to a similar conclusion, but with them it was an intellectual exercise. David Hume confesses that whenever he was forced to conclude that his empirical ego was insubstantial, he went out for a walk, had a good dinner, and forgot all about it. For these ancient sages, however, these were not logical conclusions but personal discoveries. They were actually exploring the mind, testing each level of awareness by withdrawing consciousness to the level below. In profound meditation, they found, when consciousness is so acutely focused that it is utterly withdrawn from the body and mind, it enters a kind of singularity in which the sense of a separate ego disappears. In this state, the supreme climax of meditation, the seers discovered a core of consciousness beyond time and change. They called it simply Atman, the Self.

I have described the discovery of Atman and Brahman – God immanent and God transcendent – as separate, but there is no real distinction. In the climax of meditation, the sages discovered unity: the same indivisible reality without and within. It was *advaita*, "not two." The Chandogya Upanishad says epigrammatically, *Tat tvam asi*: "Thou art That." Atman is Brahman: the Self in each person is not different from the Godhead.

Nor is it different from person to person. The Self is one, the same in every creature. This is not some peculiar tenet of the Hindu scriptures; it is the testimony of everyone who has undergone these experiments in the depths of consciousness and followed them through to the end. Here is Ruysbroeck, a great mystic of medieval Europe; every word is most carefully chosen:

> The image of God is found essentially and personally in all
> mankind. Each possesses it whole, entire and undivided,
> and all together not more than one alone. In this way we are
> all one, intimately united in our eternal image, which is the
> image of God and the source in us of all our life.

Maya

In the unitive experience, every trace of separateness disappears; life is a seamless whole. But the body cannot remain in this state for long. After a while, awareness of mind and body returns, and then the conventional world of multiplicity rushes in again with such vigor and vividness that the memory of unity, though stamped with reality, seems as distant as a dream. The unitive state has to be entered over and over until a person is established in it. But once established, even in the midst of ordinary life, one sees the One underlying the many, the Eternal beneath the ephemeral.

What is it that makes undivided reality appear to be a world of separate, transient objects? What makes each of us believe that we are the body rather than our own Self? The sages answered with a story still told after thousands of years. Imagine, they said, a man dreaming that he is being attacked by a tiger. His pulse will race, his fists will clench, his forehead will be wet with the dew of fear – all just as if the attack were real. He will be able to describe the look of his tiger, the way he smelled, the sound of his roar. For him the tiger is real, and in a sense he is not wrong: the evidence he has is not qualitatively different from the kind of evidence we trust when we are awake. People have even died from the physiological effects of a potent dream. Only when we wake up can we realize that our dream-sensations, though real to our nervous system, are a lower level of reality than the waking state.

The Upanishads delineate three ordinary states of consciousness: waking, dreaming, and dreamless sleep. Each is real, but each has a higher order of reality. For beyond these three, the Upanishads say, is the unitive state, called simply "the fourth": *turiya*. Entering this state is similar to waking up out of dream sleep: the individual passes from a lower level of reality to a higher one.

The sages called the dream of waking life – the dream of separate, merely physical existence – by a suggestive name, *maya*. In general use the word meant a kind of magic, the power of a god or sorcerer to make a thing appear to be something else. In the Gita, maya becomes the creative power of the Godhead, the primal creative energy that makes unity appear as the world of innumerable separate things with "name and form."

Later philosophers explained maya in surprisingly contemporary terms. The mind, they said, observes the so-called outside world and sees its own structure. It reports that the world consists of a multiplicity of separate objects in a framework of time, space, and causality because these are the conditions of perception. In a word, the mind looks at unity and sees diversity; it looks at what is timeless and reports transience. And in fact the percepts of its experience *are* diverse and transient; on this level of experience, separateness is real. Our mistake is in taking this for ultimate reality, like the dreamer thinking that nothing is real except his dream.

Nowhere has this "mysterious Eastern notion" been formulated more succinctly than in the epigram of Ruysbroeck: "We behold what we are, and we are what we behold." When we look at unity through the instruments of the mind, we see diversity; when the mind is transcended, we enter a higher mode of knowing – turiya, the fourth state of consciousness – in which duality disappears. This does not mean, however, that the phenomenal world is an illusion or unreal. The illusion is the sense of separateness.

Here again we can illustrate from physics: the world of "name and form" exists only as a condition of perception; at the subatomic level, separate phenomena dissolve into a flux of energy. The effect of maya is similar. The world of the senses *is* real, but it must be known for what it is: unity appearing as multiplicity.

Those who disidentify themselves with the conditions of perception in maya wake up into a higher mode of knowing in which the unity of life is apprehended directly. The disciplines for achieving this are called yoga, as is the state of union: the word comes from the root *yuj,* to yoke or bind together. The "experience" itself (properly speaking, it is beyond experience) is called *samadhi.* And the state attained is *moksha* or *nirvana,* both of which signify going beyond the conditioning of maya – time, space, and causality.

In this state we realize that we are not a physical creature but the Atman, the Self, and thus not separate from God. We see the world not as pieces but whole, and we see that whole as a manifestation of God. Once identified with the Self, we know that although the body will die, *we* will not die; our awareness of this identity is not ruptured by the death of the physical body. Thus we have realized the essential immortality which is the birthright of every human being. To such a person, the Gita says, death is no more traumatic than taking off an old coat (2:22).

Life cannot offer any higher realization. The supreme goal of human existence has been attained. The man or woman who realizes God has everything and lacks nothing: having this, "they desire nothing else, and cannot be shaken by the heaviest burden of sorrow" (6:22). Life cannot threaten such a person; all it holds is the opportunity to love, to serve, and to give.

Dharma, Karma, Rebirth, and Liberation

It has been said that if you understand just two words, *dharma* and *karma,* you will have grasped the essence of Hinduism. This is a simplification, but it would be difficult to exaggerate the importance of these concepts. Both are deeply embedded in Hindu thought, and the Gita, like other Hindu scriptures, takes them for granted, not as theoretical premises but as facts of life that can be verified in personal experience.

The word *dharma* means many things, but its underlying sense is "that which supports," from the root *dhri,* to support, hold up, or bear. Generally, *dharma* implies support from within: the essence of a thing, its virtue, that which makes it what it is.

An old story illumines this meaning with the highest ideal of Hinduism. A sage, seated beside the Ganges, notices a scorpion that has fallen into the water. He reaches down and rescues it, only to be stung. Some time later he looks down and sees the scorpion thrashing about in the water again. Once more he reaches down to rescue it, and once more he is stung. A bystander, observing all this, exclaims, "Holy one, why do you keep doing that? Don't you see that the wretched creature will only sting you in return?" "Of course," the sage replied. "It is the dharma of a scorpion to sting. But it is the dharma of a human being to save."

On a larger scale, dharma means the essential order of

things, an integrity and harmony in the universe and the affairs of life that cannot be disturbed without courting chaos. Thus it means rightness, justice, goodness, purpose rather than chance.

Underlying this idea is the oneness of life: the Upanishadic discovery that all things are interconnected because at its deepest level creation is indivisible. This oneness bestows a basic balance on the whole of nature such that any disturbance in one place has to send ripples everywhere, as a perfect bubble, touched lightly in one place, trembles all over until balance is restored. The implications are caught perfectly by those famous lines from John Donne, which deserve to be read now with a fresh eye as not merely great rhetoric but a faithful representation of reality:

> No man is an island, entire of itself; every man is a piece of the continent, a part of the main; if a clod be washed away by the sea, Europe is the less, as well as if a promontory were, as well as if a manor of thy friends or of thine own were; any man's death diminishes me, because I am involved in mankind; and therefore never send to know for whom the bell tolls, it tolls for thee.

There is an ancient Sanskrit epigram, *Ahimsa paramo dharma*: the highest dharma is *ahimsa,* nonviolence, universal love for all living creatures; for every kind of violence is a violation of dharma, the fundamental law of the unity of life.

Thus every act or thought has consequences, which themselves will have consequences; life is the most intricate web of interconnections. This is the law of karma, one of the most important and least understood ideas in ancient Indian thought. *Karma* is repeated so often in the Gita that I want to illustrate it in some detail: some intuitive sense of karma as an organic law makes Krishna's teachings a good deal clearer.

Literally, the Sanskrit *karma* means something that is done. Often it can be translated as deed or action. The law of karma states simply that every event is both a cause and an effect. Every act has consequences of a similar kind, which in turn have further consequences and so on; and every act, every karma, is also the consequence of some previous karma.

This refers not only to physical action but to mental activity as well. In their analysis of the phenomenal world and the world within, the sages of the Upanishads found that there is not merely an accidental but an essential relationship between mental and physical activity. Given appropriate conditions to develop further, thoughts breed actions of the same kind, as a seed can grow only into one particular kind of tree.

Baldly put, the law of karma says that whatever you do will come back to you. No one, of course, has the omniscience to see the picture fully. But the idea of a network of connections, far from being occult, is natural and plausible. The law of karma states unequivocally that though we cannot see the connections, we can be sure that everything that happens to us, good and bad, originated once in something we did or thought. We ourselves are responsible for what happens to us, whether or not we can understand how. It follows that we can change what happens to us by changing ourselves; we can take our destiny into our own hands.

The physical side of karma, however, only touches the surface of life. To get an inkling of how karma really works, we have to consider the mind.

Everything we do produces karma in the mind. In fact, it is in the mind rather than the world that karma's seeds are planted. Aptly, Indian philosophy compares a thought to a seed: very tiny, but it can grow into a huge, deep-rooted, wide-spreading tree. I have seen places where a seed in a crack of a pavement grew into a tree that tore up the sidewalk. It is difficult to remove such a tree, and terribly difficult to undo the effects of a lifetime of negative thinking, which can extend into many other people's lives. But it can be done, and the purpose of the Gita is to show how.

Karma is sometimes considered punitive, a matter of getting one's just desserts. This is accurate enough, but it is much more illuminating to consider karma an educative force whose purpose is to teach the individual to act in harmony with dharma – not to pursue selfish interests at the expense of others, but to contribute to life and consider the welfare of the whole. In this sense life is like a school; one can learn, one can graduate, one can skip a grade or stay behind. As long as a debt of karma remains, however, a person has to keep coming back for further education. That is the basis of samsara, the cycle of birth and death.

A good many wrong and misleading words have been written on this subject, largely because of the fascination it seems to hold in the West. Rightly understood, however, reincarnation is not exotic but quite natural. If personality consists of several sheaths, the body being only the outermost, there is no reason why personality should die when the body is shed. The sages of the Upanishads saw personality as a field of forces. Packets of karma to them are forces that have to work themselves out; if the process is interrupted by death, those forces remain until conditions allow them to work again in a new context.

Again, sleep can illustrate the dynamics of this idea. In sleep a person passes in and out of two stages, dreaming and dreamless sleep. In the first, consciousness is withdrawn from the body and senses but still engaged in the mind. In dreamless sleep, however, consciousness is withdrawn from the mind as well. Then the thinking process – even the sense of "I" – is temporarily suspended, and consciousness is said to rest in the Self. In this state a person ceases to be a separate creature, a separate personality. In dreamless sleep, the Upanishads say, a king is not a king nor a pauper poor; no one is old or young, male or female, educated or ignorant. When consciousness returns to the mind, however, the thinking process starts up again, and personality returns to the body.

According to this analysis, the ego dies every night. Every morning we pick up our desires where we left off: the same person, yet a little different too. The Upanishads describe dying as a very similar process. Consciousness is withdrawn from the body into the senses, from the senses into the mind, and finally consolidated in the ego; when the body is finally wrenched away, the ego remains, a potent package of desires and karma. And as our last waking thoughts shape our dreams, the contents of the unconscious at the time of death – the residue of all that we have thought and desired and lived for in the past – determine the context of our next life. We take a body again, the sages say, to come back to just the conditions where our desires and karma can be fulfilled. The Self-realized person, however, has no karma to work out, no personal desires; at the time of death he or she is absorbed into the Lord:

> But they for whom I am the supreme goal, who do all
> work renouncing self for me and meditate on me with
> single-hearted devotion, these I will swiftly rescue from the
> fragment's cycle of birth and death, for their consciousness
> has entered into me. (12:6–7)

Such a person, the Upanishads stress, can actually shed the body voluntarily when the hour of death arrives, by withdrawing consciousness step by step in full awareness. Some of the Gita's most fascinating verses, for those who can interpret them, are Krishna's instructions on how to die (8:12–13).

YOGA PSYCHOLOGY

In trying to describe their discoveries, the Upanishadic seers developed a specialized vocabulary. Their terms were later elaborated by mystics who were also brilliant philosophers – Kapila, Shankara, and others, the ancient Indian counterparts of authorities like Augustine and Aquinas in the West. The most useful part of this vocabulary comes from Sankhya, the philosophical system whose practical counterpart is the school of meditation called Yoga. Both are traditionally traced to one towering authority, Kapila, and have much in common with Buddhist philosophy. An ancient saying celebrates their practicality: "There is no theory like Sankhya, no practice like Yoga."

The Gita does not belong to the Sankhya school or to any other; it is as comprehensive as the Upanishads. But Sankhya provides a precise vocabulary for describing the workings of the mind, and the Gita draws on that vocabulary freely.

Sankhya philosophy posits two separate categories: *Purusha*, spirit, and *prakriti*, everything else. This is not the Western mind-matter distinction. Prakriti is the field of what can be known objectively, the field of phenomena, the world of whatever has "name and form": that is, not only of matter and energy but also of the mind. As physics postulates a unified field from which all phenomena can be derived, Sankhya describes a field that includes mental phenomena as well. Mind, energy, and matter all belong to a field of forces. Purusha, pure spirit, is the knower of this field of phenomena, and belongs to a wholly different order of reality. Only Purusha is conscious – or, rather, Purusha is consciousness itself. What we call "mind" is only an internal instrument that Purusha uses, just as the body is its external instrument. For practical purposes – at least as far as the Gita is concerned – *Purusha* may be regarded as a synonym for *Atman*. Purusha is the Self, beyond all change, the same in every creature.

Matter and Mind

Perhaps I should confess at this point that the paragraphs that follow in this short section are somewhat technical and not necessary for understanding the Gita. They can be skipped by anyone who finds them dry. I include them simply because Sankhya's explanation of mind and matter, when properly understood, makes sense of many subjects in the Gita that might otherwise seem arbitrary: maya, the survival of personality after death, the way karma works through the mind. It accommodates modern physics perfectly and offers promising explanations of mind-body relationships in health and disease. However, Sankhya's way of looking at the mind is very different from our usual physical orientation, and therefore impossible to absorb without reflection.

Sankhya's hallmark is a list (*sankhya* means counting or listing) of twenty-four principles or *tattvas* ("suchnesses") which trace the steps by which unitary, primordial prakriti becomes manifested as the countless forms of mind, matter, and energy that make up the world we live in. The tattvas are listed in the Gita:

> The field, Arjuna, is made up of the following: the five areas of sense perception; the five elements; the five sense organs and the five organs of action; the three components of the mind: *manas, buddhi,* and *ahamkara*; and the undifferentiated energy [prakriti] from which all these evolved. (13:5)

I know of no English words to use for most of these twenty-four constituents. *Manas* corresponds roughly to *mind* the way that word is commonly used; *buddhi* is the discriminative faculty, the discriminating intellect; *ahamkara*, literally "I-maker," is the sense of ego. I have used such rough labels in the translation which follows, but really they are technical terms with precise definitions, each associated with a specific function and level of consciousness. Approximations are misleading because they bring in associations from Western philosophy, which has a wholly different orientation. Behind all these categories lies a powerful, practical assumption: Sankhya is not trying to describe physical reality; it is analyzing consciousness, knowledge, for the sole purpose of unraveling the human being's true identity. So it does not begin with the material universe as something different and separate from the mind that perceives it. It does not talk about sense objects outside us and senses within and then try to get the two together. It begins with one world of experience. Sense objects and senses are not separate; they are two aspects of the same event. Mind, energy, and matter are a continuum, and the universe is not described as it might be in itself, but as it presents itself to the human mind. As they say in the "new physics," it is not just an observable universe but a participatory universe.

Let me illustrate. This morning I had a fresh mango for breakfast: a large, beautiful, fragrant one which had been allowed to ripen until just the right moment, when the skin was luminous with reds and oranges. You can see from that kind of description that I like mangoes. I must have eaten thousands of them when I was growing up, and I probably know most varieties intimately by their color, shape, flavor, fragrance, and feel.

Sankhya would say that this mango I appreciated so much does not exist in the world outside – at least, not with the qualities I ascribed to it. The mango-in-itself, for example, is not red and orange; these are categories of a nervous system that can deal only with a narrow range of radiant energy. My dog Bogart would not see a luscious red and orange mango. He would see some gray mass with no distinguishing features, much less interesting to him than a piece of buttered toast. But my mind takes in messages from five senses and fits them into a precise mango-form in consciousness, and that form – nothing outside – is what I experience. Not that there is no "real" mango! But what I experience, the objects of my sense perception and my "knowing," are in consciousness, nowhere else. A brilliant neuroscientist I was reading recently says something similar in contemporary language: we never really encounter the world; all we experience is our own nervous system.

When the Gita says that the material world is made up of five "material elements," then, it is talking about the world *as we perceive it through our five senses.* The objects of this world are in the mind, not outside. "Physical objects" in this sense require a mental component also: five "essences" or mental conditions of perception, each corresponding to one of the five senses. From these five *tanmatras* derive on the one hand the five sense organs, and on the other hand the five material elements. You can see that the number five and the correspondences of Sankhya are not arbitrary, but reflect the ways we have of sorting electrical information supplied to the brain.

Four of these elements have names similar to those from ancient philosophy in the West – earth, air, fire, and water. But if we remember that we are talking about principles of perception rather than "earth-stuff," "fire-stuff," and so on, it should become clear that this is not an antiquated theory left behind by the progress of physical science. It is quite sophisticated and accommodates contemporary physical thought rather well, for it recognizes that in the act of knowing, the mind conditions what is known.

Senses and sense objects, then, are very intimately related.

There is a causal connection, for example, between the things we see and the physical organ of seeing, the eye and its related branches of the nervous system: both depend on the underlying form in the mind that conditions how we perceive light. The objects we see are shaped by the way we see. So senses and sense objects "make sense" only together: each is incomplete without the other. That is why there is such a strong pull between senses and sense objects.

On the other hand, the Gita says, this pull has nothing to do with *us* – the Self, the knower. When Krishna keeps telling Arjuna to train his mind to be alike in pleasure and pain, he is simply being practical: to discover unity, consciousness has to be withdrawn from the hold of the senses, which ties it to duality.

> When the senses contact sense objects, a person experiences cold or heat, pleasure or pain. These experiences are fleeting; they come and go. Bear them patiently, Arjuna. Those who are not affected by these changes, who are the same in pleasure and pain, are truly wise and fit for immortality. (2:14–15)

The sensory attraction of pleasure is just an interaction between inert elements of similar stuff, very much like a magnetic pull between two objects. *We* are not involved. When I look at a fresh, ripe mango, it is natural for my senses to respond; that is their nature. But I should be able to stand aside and watch this interaction with detachment, the way people stand and watch while movers unload a van. In that way I can enjoy what my senses report without ever having to act compulsively on their likes and dislikes.

Sankhya's explanation of mind and body has profound implications for psychosomatic medicine. In a system where mental phenomena and biochemical events take place in the same field, it is much easier to account for how ways of thinking affect the body. If one idea is central to yoga psychology, it is that thoughts are real and have real, tangible consequences, as we saw in the discussion of karma. Sankhya describes thoughts as packets of potential energy, which grow more and more solid when favorable conditions are present and obstacles are removed. They become desires, then habits, then ways of living with physical consequences. Those consequences may look no more like thoughts than an oak tree looks like an acorn, but the Gita says they are just as intimately related. Just as a seed can grow into only one kind of tree, thoughts can produce effects only of the same nature. Kindness to others, to take just one example, favors a nervous system that is kind to itself.

The Forces of Evolution

Sankhya describes prakriti as a field of forces called *gunas* – a concept that gets a good deal of attention in the Gita.

According to Sankhya, the evolution of primordial prakriti

into mind and matter begins when the equilibrium of prakriti is disturbed. In Hindu myth this is the dawn of the Day of Brahma (8:17–21), a period of explosive expansion not unlike the Big Bang of modern cosmology. At this instant of creation, thrown into imbalance, prakriti differentiates itself into three basic states or qualities of primordial energy. These are the gunas. Every state of matter and mind is a combination of these three: *tamas,* inertia, *rajas,* activity, and *sattva,* harmony or equilibrium. These are only rough translations, for the gunas have no equivalent in any other philosophy I know.

The gunas can be illustrated by comparison with the three states of matter in classical physics: solid, liquid, and gas. Tamas is frozen energy, the resistance of inertia. A block of ice has a good deal of energy in the chemical bonds that hold it together, but the energy is locked in, bound up, rigid. When the ice melts, some of that energy is released as the water flows; rajas, activity, is like a swollen river, full of uncontrolled power. And sattva, harmony, can be compared with steam when its power is harnessed. These are very imprecise parallels, but they convey an important point about the gunas: all three are states of energy, and each can be converted into the others.

Guna means strand, and in the Gita the gunas are described as the very fabric of existence, the veil that hides unity in a covering of diversity. Tamas is maya's power of concealment, the darkness or ignorance that hides unitive reality; rajas distracts and scatters awareness, turning it away from reality toward the diversity of the outside world. Thus the gunas are essentially born of the mind. When the mind's activity is stilled, we see life as it is.

We can also think of the gunas as different levels of consciousness. Tamas, the lowest level, is the vast unconscious, a chaotic dumping ground for the residue of past mental states. "Unconscious" in this sense has something in common with Jung's collective unconscious, in that it is the repository not only of past experiences but also of our evolutionary heritage, the basic drives of the human being's animal past. This record is shared, of course, by all human beings, and at its deepest levels the unconscious is universal. There is no choice in tamas, no awareness; this is complete ignorance of the unity of life, ignorance of any other need than one's own basic urges.

Rajas is what we ordinarily mean by mind, the incessant stream of thought that races along, desiring, worrying, resenting, scheming, competing, frustrating and getting frustrated. Rajas is power released, but uncontrolled and egocentric.

Sattva, finally, is the so-called higher mind – detached, unruffled, self-controlled. This is not a state of repressive regulation, but the natural harmony that comes with unity of purpose, character, and desire. Negative states of mind do still come up, prompted by tamas and rajas, but there is no need to act on them.

According to Sankhya, everything in the world of mind

and matter is an expression of all three gunas, with one guna always predominant. This becomes particularly interesting in describing personality as a field of forces. The rajasic person is full of energy; the tamasic person is sluggish, indifferent, insensitive; the sattvic person, calm, resourceful, compassionate, and selfless. Yet all three are always present at some level of awareness, and their proportions change: their interplay is the dynamics of personality. The same individual will have times when he is bursting with energy and times when inertia descends and paralyzes his will, times when he is thoughtful and other times when he is moving so fast that he never notices those around him. The person is the same; he is simply experiencing the play of the gunas. As long as he identifies with his body and mind, he is at the mercy of this play. But the Self is not involved in the gunas' interaction; it is witness rather than participant:

> Without senses itself, it shines through the functioning of
> the senses. Completely independent, it supports all things.
> Beyond the gunas, it enjoys their play. (13:14)

The gunas form the basis of the most compassionate account of human nature I have come across in any philosophy or psychology, East or West. They not only explain differences in character; they describe the basic forces of personality and allow the possibility of reshaping ourselves after a higher ideal. Because personality is a process, the human being is constantly remaking himself or herself. Left to itself, the mind goes on repeating the same old habitual patterns of personality. By training the mind, however, anyone can learn to step in and change old ways of thinking; that is the central principle of yoga:

> Reshape yourself through the power of your will; never let yourself be degraded by self-will. The will is the only friend of the Self, and the will is the only enemy of the Self. (6:5)

The Gita speaks of this kind of growth as part of spiritual evolution. In its natural state, consciousness is a continuous flow of awareness. But through the distorting action of the gunas, we have fallen from this native state into fragmented, sometimes stagnant awareness. Seeing through a divided mind, we see life divided wherever we look: separate selves, antagonistic interests, conflicts within ourselves. Evolution, according to the Gita, is a painfully slow return to our native state. First tamas must be transformed into rajas – apathy and insensitiveness into energetic, enthusiastic activity. But the energy of rajas is self-centered and dispersed; it must be harnessed to a higher ideal by the will. Then it becomes sattva, when all this passionate energy is channeled into selfless action. This state is marked by happiness, a calm mind, abundant vitality, and the concentration of genius.

But even this is not the end. The goal of evolution is to return to unity: that is, to still the mind. Then the soul rests in pure, unitary consciousness, which is a state of permanent joy.

In the still mind, in the depths of meditation, the Self
reveals itself. Beholding the Self by means of the Self, an
aspirant knows the joy and peace of complete fulfillment.
(6:20)

THE ESSENCE OF THE GITA

The Gita does not present a system of philoso-
phy. It offers something to every seeker after God, of whatever
temperament, by whatever path. The reason for this universal
appeal is that it is basically practical: it is a handbook for Self-
realization and a guide to action.

Some scholars will find practicality a tall claim, because
the Gita is full of lofty and even abstruse philosophy. Yet even
its philosophy is not there to satisfy intellectual curiosity; it
is meant to explain to spiritual aspirants why they are asked
to undergo certain disciplines. Like any handbook, the Gita
makes most sense when it is practiced.

As the traditional chapter titles put it, the Gita is *brahma-
vidyayam yogashastra*, a textbook on the supreme science of
yoga. But *yoga* is a word with many meanings – as many, perhaps, as there are paths to Self-realization. What kind of yoga
does the Gita teach?

The common answer is that it presents three yogas or even
four – the four main paths of Hindu mysticism. In *jnana yoga*,
the yoga of knowledge, aspirants use their will and discrimination to disidentify themselves from the body, mind, and

senses until they know they are nothing but the Self. The followers of *bhakti yoga,* the yoga of devotion, achieve the same goal by identifying themselves completely with the Lord in love; by and large, this is the path taken by most of the mystics of Christianity, Judaism, and Islam. In *karma yoga,* the yoga of selfless action, the aspirants dissolve their identification with body and mind by identifying with the whole of life, forgetting the finite self in the service of others. And the followers of *raja yoga,* the yoga of meditation, discipline the mind and senses until the mind-process is suspended in a healing stillness and they merge in the Self.

Indians like to classify, and the eighteen chapters of the Gita are said to break into three six-chapter parts. The first third, according to this, deals with karma yoga, the second with jnana yoga, and the last with bhakti yoga: that is, the Gita begins with the way of selfless action, passes into the way of Self-knowledge, and ends with the way of love. This scheme is not tight, and non-Hindu readers may find it difficult to discover in the text. But the themes are there, and Krishna clearly shifts his emphasis as he goes on using this one word *yoga.* Here he focuses on transcendental knowledge, there on selfless action, here on meditation, there on love.

Thus the Gita offers something for every kind of spiritual aspirant, and for two thousand years each of the major schools of Indian philosophy has quoted the Gita in defense of its particular claims. This fluidity sometimes exasperates scholars, who feel the Gita contradicts itself. It also puzzled Arjuna, the faithful representative of you and me. "Krishna," he says at the beginning of chapter 3, "you've been telling me that knowledge [jnana] is better than action [karma]; so why do you urge me into such terrible action? Your words are inconsistent; they confuse me. Tell me *one* path to the highest good" (3:1–2). No doubt he speaks for every reader at this point, and for those who go on wanting one path only, the confusion simply grows worse.

For those who try to practice the Gita, however, there is a thread of inner consistency running through Krishna's advice. Like a person walking around the same object, the Gita takes more than one point of view. Whenever Krishna describes one of the traditional paths to God he looks at it from the inside, extolling its virtues over the others. For the time being, that is *the* path; when he talks about yoga, he means that one particular yoga. Thus "this ancient word" *yoga,* says Gandhi's intimate friend and secretary, Mahadev Desai,

> is pressed by the Gita into service to mean the entire gamut
> of human endeavor to storm the gates of heaven. . . . [It
> means] the yoking of all the powers of the body and the
> mind and soul to God; it means the discipline of the intel-
> lect, the mind, the emotions, the will, which such a yoking
> presupposes; it means a poise of the soul which enables one
> to look at life in all its aspects and evenly.

The Gita brings together all the specialized senses of the

word *yoga* to emphasize their common meaning: the sum of what one must do to realize the Self.

The thread through Krishna's teaching, the essence of the Gita, can be given in one word: renunciation. This is the common factor in the four yogas. It is a bleak word in English, conjuring up the austerity and self-deprivation enjoined on the monastic orders – the "poverty, chastity, and obedience" so perfectly embodied by Francis of Assisi. When the Gita promises "freedom through renunciation," the impression most of us get is that we are being asked to give up everything we want out of life; in this drab state, having lost whatever we value, we will be free from sorrow. Who wants that kind of freedom?

But this is not at all what the Gita means. It does not even enjoin material renunciation, although it certainly encourages simplicity. As always, its emphasis is on the mind. It teaches that we can become free by giving up not material things, but selfish attachments to material things – and, more important, to people. It asks us to renounce not the enjoyment of life, but the clinging to selfish enjoyment whatever it may cost others. It pleads, in a word, for the renunciation of selfishness in thought, word, and action – a theme that is common to all mystics, West and East alike.

Mahatma Gandhi encapsulates the Gita's message in one phrase: *nishkama karma,* selfless action, work free from any selfish motives. In this special sense, whatever path the Gita is presenting at a given time, it remains essentially a manual of karma yoga, for it is addressed to the person who wants to realize God without giving up an active life in the world. In the Gita the four traditional yogas are not watertight compartments, and in practice, all of them blend and support each other on the path to Self-realization.

Nishkama karma means literally work that is without *kama,* that is, without selfish desire. This word *kama* – indeed the whole idea of desire in Hindu and Buddhist psychology – is frequently misunderstood. These religions, it is sometimes held, teach an ideal of desireless action, a nirvana equated with the extinction of all desires. This drab view is far from the truth. Desire is the fuel of life; without desire nothing can be achieved, let alone so stupendous a feat as Self-realization. *Kama* is not desire; it is selfish desire. The Buddha calls it *tanha,*" thirst": the fierce, compulsive craving for personal satisfaction that demands to be slaked at any cost, whether to oneself or to others. Thus the concept also includes what Western mystics call self-will – the naked ego insisting on getting what it wants for its own gratification. The Gita teaches simply that this selfish craving is what makes a person feel separate from the rest of life. When it is extinguished – the literal meaning of *nirvana* – the mask of the transient, petty empirical ego falls, revealing our real Self.

Work hard in the world without any selfish attachment, the Gita counsels, and you will purify your consciousness of self-will. In this way any man or woman can gradually attain freedom from the bondage of selfish conditioning.

This is a *mental* discipline, not just a physical one, and I want to repeat that to understand the Gita, it is important to look beneath the surface of its injunctions and see the mental state involved. *Nishkama karma* is not "good works" or philanthropic activity; work can benefit others and still carry a substantial measure of ego involvement. Such work is good, but it is not yoga. It may benefit others, but it will not necessarily benefit the doer. Everything depends on the state of mind. Action without selfish motive purifies the mind: the doer is less likely to be ego-driven later. The same action done with a selfish motive entangles a person further, precisely by strengthening that motive so it is more likely to prompt selfish action again.

In the Gita this is said in many ways, and from differences in language it may seem that Krishna is giving different pieces of advice. In practice, however, it becomes evident that these are only various ways of saying the same thing.

To begin with, Krishna often tells Arjuna to "renounce the fruits of action" (*karma-phala*):

You have the right to work, but never to the fruit of work.
You should never engage in action for the sake of reward,
nor should you long for inaction. Perform work in this
world, Arjuna, as a man established within himself – without selfish attachments, and alike in success and defeat. For
yoga is perfect evenness of mind. (2:47–48)

"Fruits," of course, means the outcome. What Krishna means is to give up attachment to the results of what you do: that is, to give your best to every undertaking without insisting that the results work out the way you want, or even whether what you do is pleasant or unpleasant. "You have the right to action, but not to the fruits of action": each of us has the obligation to act rightly, but no power to dictate what is to come of what we do. Mahatma Gandhi explains with the authority of his personal experience:

> By detachment I mean that you must not worry whether the desired result follows from your action or not, so long as your motive is pure, your means correct. Really, it means that things will come right in the end if you take care of the means and leave the rest to Him.

"But renunciation of fruit," Gandhi warns,

> in no way means indifference to the result. In regard to every action one must know the result that is expected to follow, the means thereto, and the capacity for it. He who, being thus equipped, is without desire for the result and is yet wholly engrossed in the due fulfillment of the task before him, is said to have renounced the fruits of his action.

This attitude frees us completely. Whatever comes – success or failure, praise or blame, victory or defeat – we can give our best with a clear, unruffled mind. Nothing can shake our courage or break our will; no setback can depress us or make us feel "burned out." Clearly, as the Gita says, "Yoga is skill in action" (2:50).

Only the person who is utterly detached and utterly dedicated, Gandhi says, is free to enjoy life. Asked to sum up his life "in twenty-five words or less," he replied, "I can do it in three!" and quoted the Isha Upanishad: "Renounce and enjoy." Those who are compulsively attached to the results of action cannot really enjoy what they do; they get downcast when things do not work out and cling more desperately when they do. So the Gita classifies the karma of attachment as pleasant at first, but "bitter as poison in the end" (18:38), because of the painful bondage of conditioning.

Again, Krishna repeatedly tells Arjuna to surrender everything to him in love. But this is not different advice, merely different words. Krishna is asking Arjuna to act entirely for His sake, not for any personal gain. The whole point of the path of love is to transform motivation from "I, I, I" to "thou, thou, thou" – that is, to surrender selfish attachments by dissolving them in the desire to give.

Krishna puts this most beautifully in the famous verses of Chapter 9 which begin, "Whatever you do, make it an offering to me" (9:27). Do it, that is, not for personal reward but out of love for the Lord, present in every creature. "Whatever you eat, whatever worship you perform, whatever you give, whatever you suffer": everything is to be done and given and endured and enjoyed for the sake of the Lord in all, not for ourselves. *Manmana*: this is the refrain of the Gita. Krishna tells Arjuna repeatedly, "Fill your mind with me, focus every thought on me, think of me always"; then "you will be united with me" (see 9:34). The same injunction was given to Moses and reiterated by Jesus and Mohammed. In practical terms, it means that awareness will be integrated down to the deepest recesses of the unconscious, which is precisely the significance of the word *yoga*.

Meister Eckhart says eloquently of this state:

> Whoever has God in mind, simply and solely God, in all things, such a man carries God with him into all his works and into all places, and God alone does all his works. He seeks nothing but God; nothing seems good to him but God. He becomes one with God in every thought. Just as no multiplicity can dissipate God, so nothing can dissipate this man or make him multiple.

Thus we arrive at the idea of "actionless action": of persons so established in identification with the Self that in the midst of tireless service of those around them, they remain in inner peace, the still witness of action. They do not act, the Gita says; it is the Self that acts through them: "They alone see truly who see that all actions are performed by prakriti, while the Self remains unmoved" (13:29). Again, this is a universal testimony. Here is one of the most active of mystics, St. Catherine of Genoa:

When the soul is naughted and transformed, then of herself
she neither works nor speaks nor wills, nor feels nor hears
nor understands; neither has she of herself the feeling of
outward or inward, where she may move. And in all things
it is God who rules and guides her, without the mediation
of any creature. And the state of this soul is then a feeling of
such utter peace and tranquility that it seems to her that her
heart, and her bodily being, and all both within and without,
is immersed in an ocean of utmost peace. . . . And she is so
full of peace that though she press her flesh, her nerves, her
bones, no other thing comes forth from them than peace.

Again, when the Gita talks about "inaction in the midst
of action" (4:18, etc.), we can call on Ruysbroeck to illumine
the seeming paradox. The person who has realized God, he
says, mirrors both His aspects: "tranquility according to His
essence, activity according to His nature: absolute repose,
absolute fecundity." And he adds,

The interior person lives his life according to these two
ways; that is to say, in rest and in work. And in each of them
he is wholly and undividedly; for he dwells wholly in God
in virtue of his restful fruition and wholly in himself in
virtue of his active love. . . . This is the supreme summit of
the inner life.

This is the only kind of inaction the Gita recommends. It is
action of the most tireless kind; the only thing inactive is the
ego. To live without the daily sacrifice (*yajna*) of selfless service – to work just for oneself, or worse, to do nothing at all

– is simply to be a thief (3:12). It is not possible to do nothing, Krishna says; the very nature of the mind is incessant activity. The Gita's goal is to harness this activity in selfless service, removing the poisonous agency of the ego: "As long as one has a body, one cannot renounce action altogether. True renunciation is giving up all desire for personal reward" (18:11). Meister Eckhart explains,

> To be right, a person must do one of two things: either he must learn to have God in his work and hold fast to him there, or he must give up his work altogether. Since, however, man cannot live without activities that are both human and various, we must learn to keep God in everything we do, and whatever the job or place, keep on with him, letting nothing stand in our way.

It would be difficult to find a better summary of the Gita's message anywhere – and this, incidentally, from someone considered to represent the path of knowledge.

Krishna wraps all this up in one famous verse: "Abandon all supports and look to me for protection. I shall purify you from the sins of the past; do not grieve" (18:66). Krishna is the Self; the words mean simply to cast aside external props and dependencies and rely on the Self alone, seeking strength nowhere but within.

Why does selfless action lead to Self-realization? It is not a matter of "good" action being divinely rewarded. Self-realization is not some kind of compensation for good deeds. We can understand the dynamics if we remember that the Gita's emphasis is on the mind. Most human activity, good and bad, is tainted by ego-involvement. Such activity cannot purify consciousness, because it goes on generating new karma in the mind – in practical terms, we go on getting entangled in what we do. Selfless work purifies consciousness because when there is no trace of ego involvement, new karma is not produced; the mind is simply working out the karma it has already accumulated.

Shankara illustrates this with the simile of a potter's wheel. The ego's job is to go on incessantly spinning the wheel of the mind and making karma-pots: new ideas to act on, fresh desires to pursue. When this pointless activity stops, no more pots are made, but for a while the wheel of the mind goes on spinning out of the momentum of its past karma. This is an anguishing period in the life of every mystic: you have done everything you can; now you can only wait with a kind of impatient patience. Eventually, for no reason that one can understand, the wheel does come to a stop, dissolving the mind-process in samadhi.

A HIGHER IMAGE

Perhaps the clearest way to grasp the Gita is to look at the way it describes those who embody its teachings.

There are portraits like this at the beginning of the Gita, the middle, and the end, each offering a model of our full human potential.

The first is given at the end of chapter 2 (2:54–72), verses which Gandhi said hold the key to the entire Gita. Arjuna has just been told about Self-knowledge; now he asks a very practical question: when a person attains this knowledge, how does it show? How do such people conduct themselves in everyday life? We expect a list of virtues. Instead, Krishna delivers a surprise: the surest sign is that they have banished all selfish desires. Their senses and mind are completely trained, so they are free from sensory cravings and self-will. Identified completely with the Self, not with body or mind, they realize their immortality here on earth.

The implications of this are not spelled out; we have to see them in a living person. G. K. Chesterton once said that to understand the Sermon on the Mount, we should look not at Christ but at St. Francis. To understand the Gita I went to look at Mahatma Gandhi, who had done his best for forty years to translate those verses into his daily life. Seeing him, I understood that those "who see themselves in all and all in them" would simply not be capable of harming others. Augustine says daringly, "Love, then do as you like": nothing will come out of you but goodness. I saw too what it meant to view one's body with detachment: not indifference, but compassionate care as an instrument of service. I saw what it means to rest in the midst of intense action. Most important, I grasped one of the most refreshing ideas in Hindu mysticism: original goodness. Since the Self is the core of every personality, no one needs to acquire goodness or compassion; they are already there. All that is necessary is to remove the selfish habits that hide them.

Chapter 12 gives another portrait in its closing verses (12:13–20), and here we do get an inspiring list of the marks of those who follow the path of love:

> That one I love who is incapable of ill will, who is friendly and compassionate. Living beyond the reach of *I* and *mine* and of pleasure and pain, patient, contented, self-controlled, firm in faith, with all their heart and all their mind given to me – with such as these I am in love. (12:13–14)

And finally comes the passionate description with which the Gita ends, when Krishna tells Arjuna how to recognize the man or woman who has reached life's supreme goal:

> One who is free from selfish attachments, who has mastered himself and his passions, attains the supreme perfection of freedom from action. Listen and I shall explain now, Arjuna, how one who has attained perfection also attains Brahman, the supreme consummation of wisdom. (18:49–50)

These are not separate paths, separate ideals. All three passages describe one person: vital, active, compassionate, self-reliant in the highest sense, for he looks to the Self for every-thing and needs nothing from life but the opportunity to give. In brief, such a person knows who he is, and in that knowing is everything.

This is not running away from life, as is so often claimed. It is running *into* life, open-handed, open-armed: "flying, run-ning, and rejoicing," says Thomas à Kempis, for "he is free and will not be bound," never entangled in self-doubts, conflict, or vacillation. Far from being desireless – look at Gandhi, St. Catherine of Siena, St. Teresa, St. Francis – the man or woman who realizes God has yoked all human passions to the over-riding desire to give and love and serve; and in that unification we can see, not the extinction of personality, but its full blos-soming. This is what it means to be fully human; our ordinary lives of stimulus and response, getting and spending, seem by comparison as faint as remembered dreams. This flowering of the spirit appeals, I think, to everyone. "This is the true joy in life," says Bernard Shaw:

> the being used for a purpose recognized by yourself as a mighty one; . . . the being a force of Nature instead of a feverish selfish little clod of ailments and grievances com-plaining that the world will not devote itself to making you happy.

Instead of "Nature" with a capital *N*, of course, the Gita would say "an instrument of the Self"; but that is the only dif-ference. One of the most appealing features of the Gita for our times is that it clears up misunderstandings about the spiritual life and shows it for what it is: active, joyful, intentional, a middle path between extremes that transfigures everyday living.

FAITH AND SPIRITUAL EVOLUTION

One last untranslatable concept and I will let the Gita speak for itself. That concept is *shraddha,* and its nearest English equivalent is faith. I have translated it as such, but *shraddha* means much more. It is literally "that which is placed in the heart": all the beliefs we hold so deeply that we never think to question them. It is the set of values, axioms, prejudices, and prepossessions that colors our perceptions, governs our thinking, dictates our responses, and shapes our lives, generally without our even being aware of its presence and power.

This may sound philosophical, but shraddha is not an intellectual abstraction. It is our very substance. The Gita says, "A person is what his shraddha is" (17:3). The Bible uses almost the same words: "As a man thinketh in his heart, so is he." Shraddha reflects everything that we have made ourselves and points to what we have become. But there is nothing passive about shraddha. It is full of potency, for it prompts action, conditions behavior, and determines how we see and therefore respond to the world around us.

When Norman Cousins talks about a "belief system" analogous to the body's organ systems, that is one aspect of shraddha; he is referring to the power to heal or harm that is inherent in our ideas of ourselves. One person with a serious illness believes he has a contribution to make to the world and so he recovers; another believes his life is worthless and he dies: that is the power of shraddha. Similarly, self-image is part of shraddha. One person believes she will succeed in life and overcomes great obstacles; another, who believes she can do nothing, may be more gifted and face fewer difficulties but accomplish very little.

Yet shraddha is not brute determination or wishful thinking. When St. John of the Cross says "We live in what we love," he is explaining shraddha. This is our world. Our lives are an eloquent expression of our belief: what we deem worth having, doing, attaining, being. What we strive for shows what we value; we back our shraddha with our time, our energy, our very lives.

Thus shraddha determines destiny. As the Buddha puts it, "All that we are is the result of what we have thought. We are made of our thoughts; we are molded by our thoughts." As we think, so we become. This is true not only of individuals but of societies, institutions, and civilizations, according to the dominant ideas that shape their actions. Faith in technology, for example, is part of the shraddha of modern civilization.

"Right shraddha," according to the Gita, is faith in spiritual laws: in the unity of life, the presence of divinity in every person, the essentially spiritual nature of the human being. "Wrong shraddha" is not necessarily morally wrong, merely ignorant. It means believing that there is no more to life than physical existence, that the human being is only a biochemical entity, that happiness can be got by pursuing private interests and ignoring the rest of life. Such beliefs are misplaced: we have attached our shraddha to beliefs that life cannot bear out. Sooner or later they must prove false, and then our shraddha changes. Like our thinking, therefore – like we ourselves – shraddha evolves. The purpose of karma is to teach the consequences of shraddha, so that by trial and error, life after life, the individual soul acquires the kind of faith that leads to fulfillment of life's supreme goal. Krishna explains the dynamics:

> When a person is devoted to something with complete
> faith, I unify his faith in that. Then, when faith is completely
> unified, one gains the object of devotion. In this way, every
> desire is fulfilled by me. (7:21–22)

This is perhaps the most compassionate insight into human evolution ever expressed. The Gita is steeped in it, but it is not exclusive to the Gita or to Hinduism. "Whether you like it or not, whether you know it or not," says Meister Eckhart, "secretly Nature seeks and hunts and tries to ferret out the track in which God may be found." The whole purpose of every experience, every activity, every faculty, is to turn the human being inward and lead each of us back to our divine source. Thus every person seeking satisfaction in the world outside – pleasure, power, profit, prestige – is really looking for God: "As they approach me, so I receive them. All paths, Arjuna, lead to me" (4:11).

Two forces pervade human life, the Gita says: the upward thrust of evolution and the downward pull of our evolutionary past. Ultimately, then, the Gita is not a book of commandments but a book of choices. It does mention sin, but mostly it talks about ignorance and its consequences. Krishna tells Arjuna about the Self, the forces of the mind, the relationship between thought and action, the law of karma, and then concludes, "Now, Arjuna, reflect on these words and then do as you choose" (18:63). The struggle is between two halves of human nature, and choices are posed every moment. Everyone who has accepted this challenge, I think, will testify that life offers no fiercer battle than this war within. We have no choice about the fighting; it is built into human nature. But we do have the choice of which side to fight on:

> Remembering me, you shall overcome all difficulties through my grace. But if you will not heed me in your self-will, nothing will avail you. If you egotistically say, "I will not fight this battle," your resolve will be useless; your own nature will drive you into it. (18:58–59)

> Therefore, remember me at all times and fight on. With your heart and mind intent on me, you will surely come to me. (8:7)

Thus the Gita places human destiny entirely in human hands. Its world is not deterministic, but neither is it an expression of blind chance: we shape ourselves and our world by what we believe and think and act on, whether for good or for ill. In this sense the Gita opens not on Kurukshetra but on *dharmakshetra,* the field of dharma, where Arjuna and Krishna are standing for us all.

▯⦂

THE BHAGAVAD GITA

⦂▯

Translated by Eknath Easwaran

Chapter Introductions by Diana Morrison

1: *The War Within*

SRI KRISHNA CONSOLES and instructs Prince Arjuna as he is about to go into battle against family and friends to defend his older brother's claim to the ancient throne of the Kurus. Thus the great scripture called Bhagavad Gita, the "Song of the Lord," begins. Sri Krishna is Bhagavan, "the Lord," the mysterious incarnation of Lord Vishnu, the aspect of God who fosters and preserves the universe against the forces constantly working to destroy and corrupt it. Krishna has appeared on earth as a royal prince of the house of the Yadavas; thus he combines earthly majesty with a hidden spiritual power. Most know him only as an unimportant prince, but the wise have seen him reveal his power to destroy evil and protect the good.

The battle of the Bhagavad Gita is not Krishna's fight, however; it is Arjuna's. Krishna is only Arjuna's charioteer and advisor. He has promised Arjuna that he will be with him throughout the ordeal, but much as he passionately hopes for Arjuna's victory, he has sworn to be a noncombatant in the struggle. A charioteer's position is a lowly one compared to the status and glory of the warrior he drives, but Krishna assumes this modest role out of love for Arjuna. As charioteer, he is in a perfect position to give advice and encouragement to Arjuna without violating his promise not to join the fight himself.

To secure their claim to the throne, Arjuna and his brothers must fight not an alien army but their own cousins, who have held the kingdom for many years. Tragically, the forces against them include their own uncle, the blind king Dhritarashtra, and even the revered teachers and elders who guided Arjuna and his brothers when they were young. Arjuna, of course, wants to win the throne for his brother, who is the rightful heir to the Kuru dynasty and has endured many wrongs. But he is dismayed at the prospect of fighting his own people. Thus, on the morning the great battle is to begin, he turns to Krishna, his friend and spiritual advisor, and asks him the deeper questions about life that he has never asked before. The Bhagavad Gita is Krishna's answer.

Other warriors who appear elsewhere in the drama are mentioned in this first chapter of the Gita. To Indians these are familiar figures from the legendary past, but to most Western readers they will be unknown and even unpronounceable names. Arjuna and his brothers are known as the Pandavas, "the sons of Pandu": Yudhishthira, Bhima, Arjuna, Sahadeva, and Nakula. The other side is called the Kauravas, "the sons of Kuru." This is somewhat misleading, for both sides of the royal family are Kurus by birth. But the Pandavas are now in the position of appearing to be the dissident faction, so they are called "sons of Pandu" to distinguish them from the larger family.

Pandu was once king of the kingdom of Hastinapura, but he retired into the forest on spiritual retreat and died young. His elder brother, Dhritarashtra, was blind since birth, so he was never named ruler, but he did share power with his brother. When Pandu died his eldest son, Yudhishthira, should have succeeded him; but because Yudhishthira was only a boy, Dhritarashtra continued on after Pandu's death.

As time passed, however, Dhritarashtra's attachment to his own eldest son, Duryodhana, gradually overcame him. Instead of rising to royal impartiality and allowing Yudhishthira his fair claim, the old, blind king began to connive at his son's demand to succeed to the throne. Actually, the line of succession had grown convoluted over several generations, and it was not unthinkable that Duryodhana should rule next. But Yudhishthira's outstanding qualities and Duryodhana's corruption gradually decided the issue, at least from the moral point of view. For Duryodhana, the conflict could be resolved only on the battlefield.

Other warriors are mentioned briefly in chapter 1. Two particularly important figures in the Mahabharata story are Drona and Bhishma. Drona was born a brahmin, a member of the priestly caste, but in search of wealth he took up the way of the warrior and excelled in the knowledge of arms. He was the teacher, the guru, of all the royal princes in their youth, the sons of Pandu and the sons of Dhritarashtra alike. Thus it was he who taught both sides the skills of war – an irony which sharp-tongued Duryodhana points out in verse 3. Arjuna was Drona's best pupil when it came to the bow, excelling even Drona's own son, Ashvatthama.

Bhishma, "the grandsire" of both sides, is not actually the princes' grandfather but a respected elder statesman. As Dhritarashtra's advisor of many years' standing, he considers it his duty to stand by his king and try to protect him from his weaknesses and wrong decisions.

Another figure introduced in chapter 1 is Sanjaya, who narrates the entire Gita to the blind king Dhritarashtra. Sanjaya is not present on the battlefield, but the text tells us that the sage Vyasa, the composer of the Gita, has given him divine sight so that he can see and report everything.

Chapter 1 leaves us acutely aware that we are on a battlefield, waiting for a catastrophic war to begin; but once Krishna begins his instruction, we leave the battlefield behind and enter the realms of philosophy and mystical vision. The first chapter is but a bridge to the real subjects of the Gita, and thus need not detain us too long in our study of the poem.

Yet the first chapter has caused a great deal of debate, largely because of what it has to say about the morality of war.

Basically there have been two points of view, which are almost (but perhaps not completely) irreconcilable. First, there is the orthodox Hindu viewpoint that the Gita condones war for the warrior class: it is the *dharma,* the moral duty, of soldiers to fight in a good cause, though never for evil leaders. (It should be added that this is part of an elaborate and highly chivalrous code prescribing the just rules of war.) According to this orthodox view, the lesson of the *Mahabharata* (and therefore of the Gita) is that although war is evil, it is an evil that cannot be avoided – an evil both tragic and honorable for the warrior himself. War in a just cause, justly waged, is also in accord with the divine will. Because of this, in the Mahabharata, Yudhishthira and his noble brothers find their peace in the next world when they have finished their duty on earth.

The mystics' point of view is more subtle. For them the battle is an allegory, a cosmic struggle between good and evil. Krishna has revealed himself on earth to reestablish righteousness, and he is asking Arjuna to engage in a spiritual struggle, not a worldly one. According to this interpretation, Arjuna is asked to fight not his kith and kin but his own lower self. Mahatma Gandhi, who based his daily life on the Gita from his twenties on, felt it would be impossible to live the kind of life taught in the Gita and still engage in violence. To argue that the Gita condones violence, he said, was to give importance only to its opening verses – its preface, so to speak – and ignore the scripture itself.

For some, it helps clarify this question to look upon the Gita as an Upanishad, a mystical statement from the Vedas, that was incorporated into the warrior epic of a later age. Chapter 1 of the Gita then forms a rather perilous bridge between the warrior's world and the essential part of the Gita – Sri Krishna's revelations of spiritual truth.

– D.M.

1 □: *The War Within*

[1]O Sanjaya, tell me what happened at
Kurukshetra, the field of dharma, where my
family and the Pandavas gathered to fight.

[2]Having surveyed the forces of the Pandavas arrayed
for battle, prince Duryodhana approached his teacher,
Drona, and spoke. [3]"O my teacher, look at this mighty
army of the Pandavas, assembled by your own gifted
disciple, the son of Drupada. [4]There are heroic warriors
and great archers who are the equals of Bhima and
Arjuna: Yuyudhana, Virata, the mighty Drupada,
[5]Dhrishtaketu, Chekitana, the valiant king of Kashi,
Purujit, Kuntibhoja, the great leader Shaibya,
[6]the powerful Yudhamanyu, the valiant Uttamaujas,
and the son of Subhadra, in addition to the sons of
Draupadi. All these command mighty chariots.

⁷"O best of brahmins, listen to the names of those who are distinguished among our own forces: ⁸Bhishma, Karna, and the victorious Kripa; Ashvatthama, Vikarna, and the son of Somadatta.

⁹"There are many others, too, heroes giving up their lives for my sake, all proficient in war and armed with a variety of weapons. ¹⁰Our army is unlimited and commanded by Bhishma; theirs is small and commanded by Bhima. ¹¹Let everyone take his proper place and stand firm supporting Bhishma!"

¹²Then the powerful Bhishma, the grandsire, oldest of all the Kurus, in order to cheer Duryodhana, roared like a lion and blew his conch horn. ¹³And after Bhishma, a tremendous noise arose of conchs and cow horns and pounding on drums.

¹⁴Then Sri Krishna and Arjuna, who were standing in a mighty chariot yoked with white horses, blew their divine conchs. ¹⁵Sri Krishna blew the conch named Panchajanya, and Arjuna blew that called Devadatta. The mighty Bhima blew the huge conch Paundra. ¹⁶Yudhishthira, the king, the son of Kunti, blew the conch Anantavijaya; Nakula and Sahadeva blew their conchs as well. ¹⁷Then

the king of Kashi, the leading bowman, the great
warrior Shikhandi, Dhrishtadyumna, Virata,
the invincible Satyaki, ¹⁸Drupada, all the sons of
Draupadi, and the strong-armed son of Subhadra
joined in, ¹⁹and the noise tore through the heart
of Duryodhana's army. Indeed, the sound was
tumultuous, echoing throughout heaven and earth.

²⁰Then, O Dhritarashtra, lord of the earth,
having seen your son's forces set in their
places and the fighting about to begin, Arjuna
spoke these words to Sri Krishna:

ARJUNA

²¹O Krishna, drive my chariot between the two
armies. ²²I want to see those who desire to fight
with me. With whom will this battle be fought?
²³I want to see those assembled to fight for
Duryodhana, those who seek to please the evil-
minded son of Dhritarashtra by engaging in war.

SANJAYA

²⁴Thus Arjuna spoke, and Sri Krishna, driving his
splendid chariot between the two armies, ²⁵facing
Bhishma and Drona and all the kings of the earth,
said: "Arjuna, behold all the Kurus gathered together."

26 And Arjuna, standing between the two armies, saw fathers and grandfathers, teachers, uncles, and brothers, sons and grandsons, 27 in-laws and friends. Seeing his kinsmen established in opposition, 28 Arjuna was overcome by sorrow. Despairing, he spoke these words:

ARJUNA

O Krishna, I see my own relations here anxious to fight, 29 and my limbs grow weak; my mouth is dry, my body shakes, and my hair is standing on end. 30 My skin burns, and the bow Gandiva has slipped from my hand. I am unable to stand; my mind seems to be whirling. 31 These signs bode evil for us. I do not see that any good can come from killing our relations in battle. 32 O Krishna, I have no desire for victory, or for a kingdom or pleasures. Of what use is a kingdom or pleasure or even life, 33 if those for whose sake we desire these things – 34 teachers, fathers, sons, grandfathers, uncles, in-laws, grandsons, and others with family ties – are engaging in this battle, renouncing their wealth and their lives? 35 Even if they were to kill me, I would not want to kill them, not even to become ruler of the three worlds. How much less for the earth alone?

³⁶O Krishna, what satisfaction could we find in killing Dhritarashtra's sons? We would become sinners by slaying these men, even though they are evil. ³⁷The sons of Dhritarashtra are related to us; therefore, we should not kill them. How can we gain happiness by killing members of our own family?

³⁸Though they are overpowered by greed and see no evil in destroying families or injuring friends, we see these evils. ³⁹Why shouldn't we turn away from this sin? ⁴⁰When a family declines, ancient traditions are destroyed. With them are lost the spiritual foundations for life, and the family loses its sense of unity. ⁴¹Where there is no sense of unity, the women of the family become corrupt; and with the corruption of its women, society is plunged into chaos. ⁴²Social chaos is hell for the family and for those who have destroyed the family as well. It disrupts the process of spiritual evolution begun by our ancestors. ⁴³The timeless spiritual foundations of family and society would be destroyed by these terrible deeds, which violate the unity of life.

⁴⁴It is said that those whose family dharma has been destroyed dwell in hell. ⁴⁵This is a great sin! We are

prepared to kill our own relations out of greed for the pleasures of a kingdom. [46]Better for me if the sons of Dhritarashtra, weapons in hand, were to attack me in battle and kill me unarmed and unresisting.

SANJAYA

[47]Overwhelmed by sorrow, Arjuna spoke these words. And casting away his bow and his arrows, he sat down in his chariot in the middle of the battlefield.

CHAPTER TWO

◨: *Self-Realization*

AS ARJUNA'S SPIRITUAL teacher, Sri Krishna's task now is to rouse Arjuna from his despair and set him on the way to Self-realization.

Arjuna is essentially a man of action, renowned for his bravery, nobility, and skill in the arts of war – intelligent, but not given to reflection. Yet in his present crisis, he finds that the active life is not enough. He is forced to ask the perennial questions about life and death: Does he have a soul? Does it survive death? Is there a deeper reality than we perceive in the world around us? If so, is it possible to know it directly, and (for Arjuna is always practical) what effect does such knowing have in everyday life?

In his answer, Krishna touches on almost all the main themes and concepts of the Gita. Chapter 2 is thus a kind of overview of the sixteen chapters to come.

Sri Krishna begins by reminding Arjuna of his immortal nature: his real Self, the Atman, never dies, for it is never born; it is eternal. Thus the Gita does not lead us from stage to stage of spiritual awareness, but begins with the ultimate premise: the immortal soul is more important than the passing world.

Knowing he is out of his depth in these inner realms of the mind and spirit, Arjuna formally asks Krishna to be his spiritual teacher or *guru*. This is a basic prerequisite of a disciple's initiation in the Hindu tradition, where it is believed that virtually all seekers need the guidance of an experienced teacher. Arjuna is no exception, and he is fortunate to have Krishna himself as his guru. In the allegorical sense, Krishna is a symbol of the Atman, Arjuna's deepest Self.

This chapter introduces the idea of rebirth or *samsara*. The Self wears the body as a garment; when the garment is old, it is cast aside and a new one is put on. Thus the soul, or *jiva*, travels from life to life. Just as death is certain for the living, rebirth is certain for the dead. Krishna assures Arjuna that his basic nature is not subject to time and death; yet he reminds him that he cannot realize this truth if he cannot see beyond the dualities of life: pleasure and pain, success and failure, even heat and cold. The Gita does not teach a spirituality aimed at an enjoyable life in the hereafter, nor does it teach a way to enhance power in this life or the next. It teaches a basic detachment from pleasure and pain, as this chapter says more than once. Only in this way can an individual rise above the conditioning of life's dualities and identify with the Atman, the immortal Self.

Also, the Gita does not teach an enlightenment based on

a knowledge of the scriptures. The important thing is direct mystical experience, which Krishna will later urge Arjuna to acquire for himself.

This chapter establishes the various definitions of *yoga* taught in the Gita. Here the word does not refer to the physical postures and exercises (*hatha yoga*) it connotes in the West; it refers primarily to disciplining the mind. "Yoga is evenness of mind": detachment from the dualities of pain and pleasure, success and failure. Therefore "yoga is skill in action," because this kind of detachment is required if one is to act in freedom, rather than merely react to events compelled by conditioning. Krishna is not trying to persuade Arjuna to lead a different kind of life and renounce the world as would a monk or recluse. He tells Arjuna that if he can establish himself in yoga – in unshakable equanimity, profound peace of mind – he will be more effective in the realm of action. His judgment will be better and his vision clear if he is not emotionally entangled in the outcome of what he does.

Arjuna now asks his first question as Krishna's student. His teacher has been talking about spiritual wisdom: direct, experiential knowledge of the immortal Self. Arjuna wants to know what difference this kind of wisdom makes in everyday life. If a person establishes an ever-present awareness of the core of divinity within himself, how does it affect the way he lives? Arjuna is not interested in what people believe, but in how they conduct themselves in life.

Krishna's answer (2:55–72) is one of the most quoted passages in the Gita. Mahatma Gandhi said these verses contain the essence of the Gita: if the rest of the scripture were lost, this passage alone would be enough to teach a complete way of life. Those who are established in wisdom (*sthita-prajna*) live in continuous, unbroken awareness that they are not the perishable body but the Atman. Further, they see the same Self in everyone, for the Atman is universally present in all.

Such a one, Krishna says, does not identify with personal desires. These desires are on the surface of personality, and the Self is its very core. The Self-realized man or woman is not motivated by personal desires – in other words, by any desire for *kama*, personal satisfaction. This idea is perhaps foreign to modern ways of thinking, but basic to the Gita – and, indeed, to mystics of all traditions.

More specifically, the word *kama* refers to any gratification of the ego or the senses that entangles us in the world of samsara, and thus draws us away from the core of our being, the Self. Those established in Self-realization control their senses instead of letting their senses control them. If the senses are not controlled, Krishna warns, the mind (or emotions) will follow wherever they lead. Eventually a person following the senses loses strength of will and unity of purpose; his choices are dictated by his desires. When the will is led astray by the desire for pleasure, the mind becomes confused and scattered. Ultimately, Krishna warns, this leads to spiritual destruction:

When you keep thinking about sense objects, attachment comes. Attachment breeds desire, the lust of possession that burns to anger. Anger clouds the judgment; you can no longer learn from past mistakes. Lost is the power to choose between what is wise and what is unwise, and your life is utter waste. (2:62–63)

Yet the Gita does not recommend asceticism. It is more a matter of training the body, mind, and senses.

At the very close of the chapter, Krishna introduces the idea that it is not enough to master all selfish desires; it is also necessary to subdue possessiveness and egocentricity. If this ultimate bourne can be passed, then the seeker will know the true, immortal Self within. This is the mystics' supreme goal: knowing their real nature, they know their own immortality and realize their union with eternal Being.

– D.M.

2 ॥ *Self-Realization*

[1]These are the words that Sri Krishna spoke
to the despairing Arjuna, whose eyes were
burning with tears of pity and confusion.

KRISHNA

[2]This despair and weakness in a time of crisis are
mean and unworthy of you, Arjuna. How have you
fallen into a state so far from the path to liberation?
[3]It does not become you to yield to this weakness.
Arise with a brave heart and destroy the enemy.

ARJUNA

[4]How can I ever bring myself to fight against Bhishma
and Drona, who are worthy of reverence? How can
I, Krishna? [5]Surely it would be better to spend my
life begging than to kill these great and worthy souls!
If I killed them, every pleasure I found would be
tainted. [6]I don't even know which would be better,

for us to conquer them or for them to conquer us.
The sons of Dhritarashtra have confronted us; but
why would we care to live if we killed them?

[7]My will is paralyzed, and I am utterly confused.
Tell me which is the better path for me. Let me be
your disciple. I have fallen at your feet; give me
instruction. [8]What can overcome a sorrow that
saps all my vitality? Even power over men and
gods or the wealth of an empire seem empty.

SANJAYA

[9]This is how Arjuna, the great warrior, spoke
to Sri Krishna. With the words, "O Krishna,
I will not fight," he fell silent. [10]As they stood
between the two armies, Sri Krishna smiled and
replied to Arjuna, who had sunk into despair.

KRISHNA

[11]You speak sincerely, but your sorrow has no
cause. The wise grieve neither for the living nor
for the dead. [12]There has never been a time when
you and I and the kings gathered here have not
existed, nor will there be a time when we will
cease to exist. [13]As the same person inhabits the
body through childhood, youth, and old age, so

too at the time of death he attains another body.
The wise are not deluded by these changes.

¹⁴When the senses contact sense objects, a person
experiences cold or heat, pleasure or pain. These
experiences are fleeting; they come and go.
Bear them patiently, Arjuna. ¹⁵Those who are
unaffected by these changes, who are the same
in pleasure and pain, are truly wise and fit for
immortality. Assert your strength and realize this!

¹⁶The impermanent has no reality; reality lies in the
eternal. Those who have seen the boundary between
these two have attained the end of all knowledge.
¹⁷Realize that which pervades the universe and is
indestructible; no power can affect this unchanging,
imperishable reality. ¹⁸The body is mortal, but
that which dwells in the body is immortal and
immeasurable. Therefore, Arjuna, fight in this battle.

¹⁹One believes he is the slayer, another believes he
is the slain. Both are ignorant; there is neither slayer
nor slain. ²⁰You were never born; you will never
die. You have never changed; you can never change.
Unborn, eternal, immutable, immemorial, you do
not die when the body dies. ²¹Realizing that which

is indestructible, eternal, unborn, and unchanging, how can you slay or cause another to slay?

22As one abandons worn-out clothes and acquires new ones, so when the body is worn out a new one is acquired by the Self, who lives within.

23The Self cannot be pierced by weapons or burned by fire; water cannot wet it, nor can the wind dry it. 24The Self cannot be pierced or burned, made wet or dry. It is everlasting and infinite, standing on the motionless foundations of eternity. 25The Self is unmanifested, beyond all thought, beyond all change. Knowing this, you should not grieve.

26O mighty Arjuna, even if you believe the Self to be subject to birth and death, you should not grieve. 27Death is inevitable for the living; birth is inevitable for the dead. Since these are unavoidable, you should not sorrow. 28Every creature is unmanifested at first and then attains manifestation. When its end has come, it once again becomes unmanifested. What is there to lament in this?

29The glory of the Self is beheld by a few, and a few describe it; a few listen, but many

without understanding. [30]The Self of all beings,
living within the body, is eternal and cannot
be harmed. Therefore, do not grieve.

[31]Considering your dharma, you should not
vacillate. For a warrior, nothing is higher than a
war against evil. [32]The warrior confronted with
such a war should be pleased, Arjuna, for it comes
as an open gate to heaven. [33]But if you do not
participate in this battle against evil, you will incur
sin, violating your dharma and your honor.

[34]The story of your dishonor will be repeated
endlessly: and for a man of honor, dishonor is
worse than death. [35]These brave warriors will
think you have withdrawn from battle out of fear,
and those who formerly esteemed you will treat
you with disrespect. [36]Your enemies will ridicule
your strength and say things that should not be
said. What could be more painful than this?

[37]Death means the attainment of heaven; victory
means the enjoyment of the earth. Therefore
rise up, Arjuna, resolved to fight! [38]Having
made yourself alike in pain and pleasure, profit

and loss, victory and defeat, engage in this
great battle and you will be freed from sin.

[39]You have heard the intellectual explanation of
Sankhya, Arjuna; now listen to the principles
of yoga. By practicing these you can break
through the bonds of karma. [40]On this path
effort never goes to waste, and there is no failure.
Even a little effort toward spiritual awareness
will protect you from the greatest fear.

[41]Those who follow this path, resolving deep within
themselves to seek me alone, attain singleness
of purpose. For those who lack resolution, the
decisions of life are many-branched and endless.

[42]There are ignorant people who speak flowery
words and take delight in the letter of the law,
saying that there is nothing else. [43]Their hearts
are full of selfish desires, Arjuna. Their idea of
heaven is their own enjoyment, and the aim of
all their activities is pleasure and power. The
fruit of their actions is continual rebirth. [44]Those
whose minds are swept away by the pursuit of
pleasure and power are incapable of following
the supreme goal and will not attain samadhi.

⁴⁵The scriptures describe the three gunas. But
you should be free from the action of the gunas,
established in eternal truth, self-controlled, without
any sense of duality or the desire to acquire and hoard.

⁴⁶Just as a reservoir is of little use when the
whole countryside is flooded, scriptures
are of little use to the illumined man or
woman, who sees the Lord everywhere.

⁴⁷You have the right to work, but never to the
fruit of work. You should never engage in action
for the sake of reward, nor should you long for
inaction. ⁴⁸Perform work in this world, Arjuna,
as a man established within himself – without
selfish attachments, and alike in success and
defeat. For yoga is perfect evenness of mind.

⁴⁹Seek refuge in the attitude of detachment and
you will amass the wealth of spiritual awareness.
Those who are motivated only by desire for the
fruits of action are miserable, for they are constantly
anxious about the results of what they do. ⁵⁰When
consciousness is unified, however, all vain anxiety
is left behind. There is no cause for worry, whether

things go well or ill. Therefore, devote yourself to
the disciplines of yoga, for yoga is skill in action.

51The wise unify their consciousness and
abandon attachment to the fruits of action,
which binds a person to continual rebirth.
Thus they attain a state beyond all evil.

52When your mind has overcome the confusion of
duality, you will attain the state of holy indifference
to things you hear and things you have heard.
53When you are unmoved by the confusion of
ideas and your mind is completely united in deep
samadhi, you will attain the state of perfect yoga.

ARJUNA

54Tell me of those who live established in
wisdom, ever aware of the Self, O Krishna. How
do they talk? How sit? How move about?

KRISHNA

55They live in wisdom who see themselves in all
and all in them, who have renounced every selfish
desire and sense craving tormenting the heart.

⁵⁶Neither agitated by grief nor hankering after pleasure, they live free from lust and fear and anger. Established in meditation, they are truly wise. ⁵⁷Fettered no more by selfish attachments, they are neither elated by good fortune nor depressed by bad. Such are the seers.

⁵⁸Even as a tortoise draws in its limbs, the wise can draw in their senses at will. ⁵⁹Aspirants abstain from sense pleasures, but they still crave for them. These cravings all disappear when they see the highest goal. ⁶⁰Even of those who tread the path, the stormy senses can sweep off the mind. ⁶¹They live in wisdom who subdue their senses and keep their minds ever absorbed in me.

⁶²When you keep thinking about sense objects, attachment comes. Attachment breeds desire, the lust of possession that burns to anger. ⁶³Anger clouds the judgment; you can no longer learn from past mistakes. Lost is the power to choose between what is wise and what is unwise, and your life is utter waste. ⁶⁴But when you move amidst the world of sense, free from attachment and aversion alike, ⁶⁵there comes the peace in which all sorrows end, and you live in the wisdom of the Self.

⁶⁶The disunited mind is far from wise; how can
it meditate? How be at peace? When you know
no peace, how can you know joy? ⁶⁷When you
let your mind follow the call of the senses, they
carry away your better judgment as storms
drive a boat off its charted course on the sea.

⁶⁸Use all your power to free the senses from
attachment and aversion alike, and live in the full
wisdom of the Self. ⁶⁹Such a sage awakes to light
in the night of all creatures. That which the world
calls day is the night of ignorance to the wise.

⁷⁰As rivers flow into the ocean but cannot make
the vast ocean overflow, so flow the streams of the
sense-world into the sea of peace that is the sage.
But this is not so with the desirer of desires.

⁷¹They are forever free who renounce all
selfish desires and break away from the ego-
cage of "I," "me," and "mine" to be united with
the Lord. ⁷²This is the supreme state. Attain to
this, and pass from death to immortality.

❏: *Selfless Service*

THE TITLE OF this chapter in Sanskrit is Karma Yoga, "The Way of Action," and here we take an apparently sharp turn away from the subject of the previous chapter. In fact, Arjuna changes the subject completely. Krishna has been trying to convince him that he has an immortal soul, but Arjuna continues to worry about his immediate predicament. It is not that he is uninterested in mystical enlightenment, but his main concern at the moment is just what he is supposed to do next.

Or, he asks, perhaps what he does is not so important after all. Has Krishna been telling him to concentrate on acquiring spiritual wisdom and to forget about his apparent duties in the world?

Krishna replies that there is no way Arjuna can avoid the obligation of selfless action, or karma yoga. Arjuna must act selflessly, out of a sense of duty. He must work not for his own sake, but for the welfare of all. Krishna points out that this is a basic law underlying all creation. Each being must do its part in the grand scheme of things, and there is no way to avoid this obligation – except perhaps by the complete enlightenment which loosens all the old bonds of karma.

Here the Gita refers to the doctrine of karma, one of the basic teachings in all Hindu and Buddhist scriptures. *Karma* literally means deed or action; what is sometimes called the "law of karma" refers to an underlying law of cause and effect that is seen to permeate all existence. The idea is that every action leads to a reasonable result – and, consequently, that everything that happens can be traced to something done in the past. Actions determine destiny: this is the basic idea of karma. If anything happens to us that is truly good, we must have done something in the past to deserve it; if something ill befalls us, then at some time in the past we did something that was not so meritorious. This is a basic moral law that all great spiritual traditions share: the belief that we reap what we sow.

The Hindu tradition gave a great deal of thought to this problem of moral cause and effect, and generation after generation of spiritual teachers fathomed its depths and implications. One fear that developed over time was that all action was in a sense an open door to bondage: anything a person did would bind him to the endless cycle of cause and effect. Some "fruits" of action would of course be pleasant – not all karma is painful. But even this pleasure could be a trap, because we would seek it compulsively, tying ourselves tighter and tighter to the responsibilities and opportunities of the worldly life and forgetting our spiritual dimension altogether.

In chapter 3 Krishna begins to tell Arjuna the way out of this maze of cause and effect. It is not to avoid work, especially the duties required by his station in life, but to perform those duties without selfish attachment to their "fruit," or outcome. If Arjuna follows this path of selfless work, Krishna explains, he will enjoy this world as well as the next. More important, he will gain a spiritual blessing and will be lessening his debt of karma. Only when he is free from every bond of karma – every consequence of past action – can he achieve life's ultimate goal.

The world is bound in its own activity, for all creatures except the illumined man or woman work for their own pleasure and gain. Because they act selfishly, they are bound by the results, whether good or bad. We must act in a selfless spirit, Krishna says, without ego-involvement and without getting entangled in whether things work out the way we want; only then will we not fall into the terrible net of karma. We cannot hope to escape karma by refraining from our duties: even to survive in the world, we must act.

True, the Hindu scriptures do hold out another path – *jnana yoga,* the path of wisdom – which does not enjoin action. But Krishna does not really offer this to Arjuna as an alternative; it is acknowledged and then dropped. Perhaps

Krishna knows that Arjuna is not the type to disengage himself and go off on a search for the mystical vision. For Arjuna, the active life is essential.

The danger, of course, of a life of active engagement in the world is that Arjuna will get caught up in his actions and begin to act out of selfish motives. If this were to happen, he would be doomed to spiritual failure.

Having a good deal of self-knowledge, Arjuna senses this danger. He asks Krishna a fundamental question: What power binds us to our selfish ways? Even if we wish to act rightly, so often we do the wrong thing. What power moves us?

Krishna replies that anger and selfish desire are our greatest enemies. They are the destructive powers that can compel us to wander away from our purpose, to end up in self-delusion and despair.

Here it is necessary to introduce two technical terms from Hindu philosophy. The Gita is not an academic work of philosophy, but a poetic, practical text. Still, it does refer from time to time to Sankhya, one of the six traditional schools of Indian philosophy. In Sankhya, the phenomenal world of mind and matter is described as having three basic qualities or *gunas*: *sattva*– goodness, light, purity; *rajas*– passion, activity, energy; and *tamas*– darkness, ignorance, inertia. According to Sankhya, spiritual evolution progresses from tamas to rajas to sattva, and final liberation takes the soul beyond the three gunas altogether.

Here Krishna warns Arjuna to beware the pitfalls of rajas, for it is from rajas that anger and selfish desire arise. Arjuna must realize that his true nature, the Atman, is above entanglement in the gunas. The gunas act and react upon one another, but Arjuna's inner being is not affected. If he cannot reach this detachment, he will be always caught in the emotional storms of passion (rajas) or the quagmires of inertia (tamas) which alternate in dominating the mind and body.

Krishna offers Arjuna the example of King Janaka, well known from holy legend, as a model for the princely estate. Janaka was a king who ruled well and did not shirk his responsibilities, yet he was detached and worked from a sense of duty, not for personal gain or enjoyment. He was revered as a royal sage who pursued his enlightenment not by renouncing the world, but by working in it and contributing to its welfare, thus enjoying the best of both worlds.

– D.M.

3 ୴ *Selfless Service*

ARJUNA

¹O Krishna, you have said that knowledge is greater than action; why then do you ask me to wage this terrible war? ²Your advice seems inconsistent. Give me one path to follow to the supreme good.

KRISHNA

³At the beginning of time I declared two paths for the pure heart: *jnana yoga,* the contemplative path of spiritual wisdom, and *karma yoga,* the active path of selfless service.

⁴One who shirks action does not attain freedom; no one can gain perfection by abstaining from work. ⁵Indeed, there is no one who rests for even an instant; all creatures are driven to action by their own nature.

⁶Those who abstain from action while allowing the mind to dwell on sensual pleasure cannot

be called sincere spiritual aspirants. ⁷But they
excel who control their senses through the
mind, using them for selfless service.

⁸Fulfill all your duties; action is better than inaction.
Even to maintain your body, Arjuna, you are obliged
to act. ⁹Selfish action imprisons the world. Act
selflessly, without any thought of personal profit.

¹⁰At the beginning, mankind and the obligation
of selfless service were created together.
"Through selfless service, you will always
be fruitful and find the fulfillment of your
desires": this is the promise of the Creator.

¹¹Honor and cherish the devas as they honor and
cherish you; through this honor and love you will
attain the supreme good. ¹²All human desires are
fulfilled by the devas, who are pleased by selfless
service. But anyone who enjoys the things given by the
devas without offering selfless acts in return is a thief.

¹³The spiritually minded, who eat in the spirit of
service, are freed from all their sins; but the selfish,
who prepare food for their own satisfaction, eat sin.
¹⁴Living creatures are nourished by food, and food

is nourished by rain; rain itself is the water of life, which comes from selfless worship and service.

¹⁵Every selfless act, Arjuna, is born from Brahman, the eternal, infinite Godhead. Brahman is present in every act of service. ¹⁶All life turns on this law, O Arjuna. Those who violate it, indulging the senses for their own pleasure and ignoring the needs of others, have wasted their life. ¹⁷But those who realize the Self are always satisfied. Having found the source of joy and fulfillment, they no longer seek happiness from the external world. ¹⁸They have nothing to gain or lose by any action; neither people nor things can affect their security.

¹⁹Strive constantly to serve the welfare of the world; by devotion to selfless work one attains the supreme goal of life. ²⁰Do your work with the welfare of others always in mind. It was by such work that Janaka attained perfection; others too have followed this path.

²¹What the outstanding person does, others will try to do. The standards such people create will be followed by the whole world. ²²There is nothing in the three worlds for me to gain, Arjuna, nor is there

anything I do not have; I continue to act, but I am not driven by any need of my own. ²³If I ever refrained from continuous work, everyone would immediately follow my example. ²⁴If I stopped working I would be the cause of cosmic chaos, and finally of the destruction of this world and these people.

²⁵The ignorant work for their own profit, Arjuna;
the wise work for the welfare of the world,
without thought for themselves. ²⁶By abstaining
from work you will confuse the ignorant,
who are engrossed in their actions. Perform
all work carefully, guided by compassion.

²⁷All actions are performed by the gunas of prakriti. Deluded by identification with the ego, a person thinks, "*I* am the doer." ²⁸But the illumined man or woman understands the domain of the gunas and is not attached. Such people know that the gunas interact with each other; they do not claim to be the doer.

²⁹Those who are deluded by the operation of
the gunas become attached to the results of
their action. Those who understand these truths
should not unsettle the ignorant. ³⁰Performing
all actions for my sake, completely absorbed

in the Self, and without expectations, fight!
– but stay free from the fever of the ego.

[31]Those who live in accordance with these divine
laws without complaining, firmly established in
faith, are released from karma. [32]Those who violate
these laws, criticizing and complaining, are utterly
deluded, and are the cause of their own suffering.

[33]Even the wise act within the limitations of their
own nature. Every creature is subject to prakriti;
what is the use of repression? [34]The senses have
been conditioned by attraction to the pleasant
and aversion to the unpleasant. Do not be ruled
by them; they are obstacles in your path.

[35]It is better to strive in one's own dharma than to
succeed in the dharma of another. Nothing is ever
lost in following one's own dharma, but competition
in another's dharma breeds fear and insecurity.

ARJUNA

[36]What is the force that binds us to selfish
deeds, O Krishna? What power moves us,
even against our will, as if forcing us?

KRISHNA

[37]It is selfish desire and anger, arising from
the guna of rajas; these are the appetites and
evils which threaten a person in this life.

[38]Just as a fire is covered by smoke and a mirror is
obscured by dust, just as the embryo rests deep within
the womb, knowledge is hidden by selfish desire
– [39]hidden, Arjuna, by this unquenchable fire for
self-satisfaction, the inveterate enemy of the wise.

[40]Selfish desire is found in the senses, mind,
and intellect, misleading them and burying
the understanding in delusion. [41]Fight
with all your strength, Arjuna! Controlling
your senses, conquer your enemy, the
destroyer of knowledge and realization.

[42]The senses are higher than the body, the mind
higher than the senses; above the mind is the
intellect, and above the intellect is the Atman.
[43]Thus, knowing that which is supreme, let the
Atman rule the ego. Use your mighty arms to
slay the fierce enemy that is selfish desire.

ॐ: *Wisdom in Action*

KRISHNA IS EAGER to grant Arjuna knowledge of the highest spiritual truths, or even a rare mystical vision; but Arjuna has been asking for Krishna to simply get him out of his present difficulties. Of course these difficulties are not minor – he is caught in a family tragedy that has developed into a vicious conflict. If he cannot extricate himself, he knows that he will have to take part in a catastrophic battle that no one wants.

So when Krishna begins to tell Arjuna about the "secret teachings" he will be privileged to hear because he is Krishna's favorite devotee and friend, it hardly registers in Arjuna's consciousness. His reply is confused. "How could you have taught any secret wisdom to the sages of old?" he asks.

At this point Krishna reminds Arjuna again of the process of rebirth. They have both been reborn many times, but naturally Arjuna does not remember his past lives because he has no access to this kind of knowledge. Krishna remembers his former births, but he is no ordinary being. He reveals that he has chosen to take on human birth many times for the welfare of the world. Whenever dharma, the law of life's unity, declines, he wraps himself in his maya and takes on a finite form. Thus he returns age after age.

Vishnu, the preserving or sustaining person of the Hindu Trinity, is not mentioned here, but Krishna is usually looked upon as an incarnation of this aspect of God. As the Lord, Krishna explains, he dwells in every being, but he is manifested with special power in his incarnations or *avatars*. *Avatara* literally means descent: Vishnu is believed to descend and incarnate himself on earth from age to age to reestablish divine law (dharma). Without such intervention the entire created universe would go into decline. The natural course of creation is to go through cycles of regeneration and decay, but Vishnu – Krishna – has compassion for all the suffering of the world, and comes himself to protect the good and destroy evil. Thus Vishnu has a special relationship with all beings: he personifies the aspect of God who so loves the world that he comes into it to reestablish the purity and happiness of the Golden Age.

Krishna here reveals a little of his hidden, divine nature. He tells Arjuna that mystical union with him is possible through devotion, by which one can enter the state of divine love in which one sees God in every creature. Krishna also takes on the role of creator. It is he who has patterned the world along the lines of guna and karma.

This mystic aspect of Krishna's being dominates the Gita. In the *Mahabharata,* Krishna is a princely ally who is wise and daring in his support of his friend Arjuna. But the author of the Gita is not concerned with this Krishna; he turns his attention to the mystery of Krishna's divine nature as an aspect of Vishnu. In this sense Krishna is the inner Self in all beings. His name comes from the Sanskrit root *krish,* "to draw to oneself, to attract." He is the "attractive one," the "Lord of loving attraction." By another etymology, the word *Krishna* means "the dark one." The author of the Gita sees revealed in him the ultimate Godhead, the supreme being. But this reality is often veiled, and then Krishna is seen as an ordinary human being – or, rather, as an exceptionally gifted man, but not as God.

Many of Krishna's words make most sense when we realize that when he speaks of himself, he is often not describing a transcendental reality so much as trying to tell Arjuna about the Self in every human being. When he says, for example, "Actions do not cling to me because I am not attached to their results," he means, "Arjuna, actions do not cling to your real Self." The Self in us is not touched by action; whatever we do, it remains unsullied. "Those who understand this" – about themselves – "and practice it live in freedom."

The latter part of this chapter turns from lofty mystical topics back to Arjuna's immediate problem. Krishna begins to talk about action, and work, and things that should be done and should not be done. It is essential, he reminds Arjuna, to act wisely, with detachment. The wise never act with selfish attachment to the fruit of their labor; they give their best in fortune and misfortune alike. Such people act in freedom.

The next section deals with the various kinds of *yajna* – worship or offering – that may be performed by spiritual aspirants of differing temperaments. Hindu rituals often involve making an offering to the gods by pouring an oblation into the sacred fire. Here the image is the same: whatever is offered is symbolically thrown into a consuming fire that carries the offering to God. The offering may be as obvious as worldly goods, or as subtle as knowledge or meditation: in any case it requires a measure of self-sacrifice. Yajna is a basic action, necessary to life, and those who do not perform some kind of selfless service find no home in this world or the next.

The final verses of chapter 4 introduce a new principle. In the last chapter, Krishna mentioned the path of spiritual wisdom as an alternative to the path of action or karma yoga. Now he reveals that wisdom is the goal of selfless action: knowing is the fruit of doing. The goal of all karma yoga or yajna is liberation and spiritual wisdom. The fire of spiritual awareness burns to ashes even a great heap of karma; thus true knowledge is the greatest purifier of the soul.

Krishna ends by exhorting Arjuna to cut through the doubts that still stifle him. This is the first – but not the last – mention that Krishna makes of Arjuna's doubting heart. There has been no indication so far that Arjuna has taken in and accepted Krishna's words. But even though Arjuna continues to drag his feet, Krishna does not abandon him.

– D.M.

4 �II: *Wisdom in Action*

KRISHNA

¹I told this eternal secret to Vivasvat. Vivasvat
taught Manu, and Manu taught Ikshvaku. ²Thus,
Arjuna, eminent sages received knowledge of
yoga in a continuous tradition. But through time
the practice of yoga was lost in the world.

³The secret of these teachings is profound.
I have explained them to you today because
you are my friend and devotee.

ARJUNA

⁴You were born much after Vivasvat; he
lived very long ago. Why do you say that
you taught this yoga in the beginning?

KRISHNA

⁵You and I have passed through many births, Arjuna.
You have forgotten, but I remember them all.

⁶My true being is unborn and changeless. I am the
Lord who dwells in every creature. Through the power
of my own maya, I manifest myself in a finite form.

⁷Whenever dharma declines and the purpose
of life is forgotten, I manifest myself on earth.
⁸I am born in every age to protect the good,
to destroy evil, and to reestablish dharma.

⁹Those who know me as their own divine Self break
through the belief that they are the body and are not
reborn as separate creatures. Such a one, Arjuna, is
united with me. ¹⁰Delivered from selfish attachment,
fear, and anger, filled with me, surrendering
themselves to me, purified in the fire of my being,
many have reached the state of unity in me.

¹¹As they approach me, so I receive them.
All paths, Arjuna, lead to me.

¹²Those desiring success in their actions worship
the gods; through action in the world of mortals,
their desires are quickly fulfilled. ¹³The distinctions
of caste, guna, and karma have come from me. I am
their cause, but I myself am changeless and beyond
all action. ¹⁴Actions do not cling to me because I am

not attached to their results. Those who understand this and practice it live in freedom. ¹⁵Knowing this truth, aspirants desiring liberation in ancient times engaged in action. You too can do the same, pursuing an active life in the manner of those ancient sages.

¹⁶What is action and what is inaction? This question has confused the greatest sages. I will give you the secret of action, with which you can free yourself from bondage. ¹⁷The true nature of action is difficult to grasp. You must understand what is action and what is inaction, and what kind of action should be avoided.

¹⁸The wise see that there is action in the midst of inaction and inaction in the midst of action. Their consciousness is unified, and every act is done with complete awareness.

¹⁹The awakened sages call a person wise when all his undertakings are free from anxiety about results; all his selfish desires have been consumed in the fire of knowledge. ²⁰The wise, ever satisfied, have abandoned all external supports. Their security is unaffected by the results of their action; even while acting, they really do nothing at all. ²¹Free from

expectations and from all sense of possession, with mind and body firmly controlled by the Self, they do not incur sin by the performance of physical action.

²²They live in freedom who have gone beyond the dualities of life. Competing with no one, they are alike in success and failure and content with whatever comes to them. ²³They are free, without selfish attachments; their minds are fixed in knowledge. They perform all work in the spirit of service, and their karma is dissolved.

²⁴The process of offering is Brahman; that which is offered is Brahman. Brahman offers the sacrifice in the fire of Brahman. Brahman is attained by those who see Brahman in every action.

²⁵Some aspirants offer material sacrifices to the gods. Others offer selfless service as sacrifice in the fire of Brahman. ²⁶Some renounce all enjoyment of the senses, sacrificing them in the fire of sense restraint. Others partake of sense objects but offer them in service through the fire of the senses. ²⁷Some offer the workings of the senses and the vital forces through the fire of self-control, kindled in the path of knowledge.

²⁸Some offer wealth; others offer sense restraint
and suffering. Some take vows and offer knowledge
and study of the scriptures; and some make the
offering of meditation. ²⁹Some offer the forces of
vitality, regulating their inhalation and exhalation,
and thus gain control over these forces. ³⁰Others
offer the forces of vitality through restraint of
their senses. All these understand the meaning of
service and will be cleansed of their impurities.

³¹True sustenance is in service, and through it
a man or woman reaches the eternal Brahman.
But those who do not seek to serve are without
a home in this world. Arjuna, how can they
be at home in any world to come?

³²These offerings are born of work, and each guides
mankind along a path to Brahman. Understanding
this, you will attain liberation. ³³The offering of
wisdom is better than any material offering, Arjuna;
for the goal of all work is spiritual wisdom.

³⁴Approach those who have realized the purpose of
life and question them with reverence and devotion;
they will instruct you in this wisdom. ³⁵Once you

attain it, you will never again be deluded. You
will see all creatures in the Self, and all in me.

[36]Even if you were the most sinful of sinners, Arjuna,
you could cross beyond all sin by the raft of spiritual
wisdom. [37]As the heat of a fire reduces wood to
ashes, the fire of knowledge burns to ashes all karma.
[38]Nothing in this world purifies like spiritual wisdom.
It is the perfection achieved in time through the path
of yoga, the path which leads to the Self within.

[39]Those who take wisdom as their highest
goal, whose faith is deep and whose senses are
trained, attain wisdom quickly and enter into
perfect peace. [40]But the ignorant, indecisive
and lacking in faith, waste their lives. They can
never be happy in this world or any other.

[41]Those established in the Self have renounced
selfish attachments to their actions and cut
through doubts with spiritual wisdom. They act
in freedom. [42]Arjuna, cut through this doubt
in your own heart with the sword of spiritual
wisdom. Arise; take up the path of yoga!

❒: *Renounce & Rejoice*

AT THE BEGINNING of this chapter, the traditional approach to the spiritual life – that is, "leaving the world," retiring from the ordinary affairs of job and family – is contrasted with working in the world with detachment. The general term for retiring from the world is *sannyasa,* "renunciation." Traditionally, sannyasa meant renouncing all worldly ties and attachments. The person undertaking the vow of sannyasa would leave home, family, and occupation to pursue a strict contemplative life.

This was a path chosen by very few, even in ancient India. Yet we shouldn't forget that surprising numbers of people in traditional societies, both in the East and the West, have chosen a monastic life removed from the turmoil of the world. In India, the Compassionate Buddha provides the classic example of one who leaves the comforts and fulfillments of family and worldly life to seek the lonely way to Self-realization. The story is well known throughout Asia. Siddhartha Gautama was a prince with every worldly satisfaction within his reach, who left his palace to find a way to lead the world beyond suffering and death. He became a wandering *sannyasi,* a lonely, austere monk. Only after he had attained to complete enlightenment did he return to society, to teach others of the peace of nirvana.

Though Krishna acknowledges here that this way of sannyasa can lead to the goal, he recommends the path of selfless action or selfless service as the better way. He contrasts the way of Sankhya – which in this context means knowledge of the Self in a general way – to the way of yoga, which here means the way of action. This term *yoga* presents difficulties in the Gita because it means different things at different times, and many definitions are given of this all-purpose term. But for several chapters the topic under discussion has been the active spiritual life, or karma yoga, and that is clearly what is meant in this context. *Sankhya* and *yoga* might also be translated as "theory and practice."

It would seem that at the time of the Gita the path of wisdom was regarded very highly, while the path of action may have been looked upon as an adulteration of the spiritual life. It is even possible that the Gita was the first Hindu scripture to introduce the novel idea of combining karma yoga with the pursuit of Self-knowledge. Krishna says that only immature, inexperienced people look upon the paths of knowledge and action as different. The true goal of action is knowledge of the

Self. Following either path faithfully will lead to the complete spiritual vision.

It is essential in karma yoga that the selfish ego not expect gratification from the work. When there is no selfish involvement in work, the worker does not come to spiritual harm. The example is the lotus: it spends its life floating in water, yet the drops of water roll off its leaves without ever wetting them. Similarly, as long as the karma yogis do not expect reward or recognition, any evil that might stain them has nowhere to cling. Such yogis are said to be detached from the outcome or fruits of their actions (*karma phala*).

Krishna warns Arjuna that a life of work, even successful work, cannot be fulfilling without Self-knowledge. Ultimately, the true Self within him is not affected by what he does, whether good or bad. Only knowledge of the Self, which rises like the sun at dawn, can fulfill the purpose of his life and lead him beyond rebirth.

This knowledge of the Self or Atman is, by its very nature, also knowledge of Brahman, the all-pervading, immanent and transcendent Godhead. Krishna says that the illumined person sees this divine essence in all beings. He or she has "equal vision" and sees the divine Self in all, regardless of the outer aspect.

The last three verses of the chapter describe a state of profound meditation called samadhi. When meditation becomes very deep, breathing becomes slow, steady, and even, and the windows of the senses close to all outward sensations. Next the faculties of the mind quiet down, resting from their usually frantic activity; even the primal emotions of desire, fear, and anger subside. When all these sensory and emotional tides have ceased to flow, then the spirit is free, *mukta* – at least for the time being. It has entered the state called samadhi.

Samadhi can come and go; generally it can be entered only in a long period of meditation and after many years of ardent endeavor. But one verse (5:28) adds the significant word *sada,* "always." Once this state of deep concentration becomes established, the person lives in spiritual freedom, or *moksha,* permanently. This is extremely rare. Mystics of the West as well as the East have attained brief glimpses of unity, but very few can be said to have dwelt in it permanently, as if it were their natural habitat. In the West the most prominent figures are Meister Eckhart, St. Teresa of Avila, and St. John of the Cross, though there have been others. In the Hindu tradition there is a long line of saints and mystics who have tried to communicate something of the nature of this union with Reality or God, from the unknown recorders of the Upanishads through the Buddha, Shankara, and Meera, to Ramakrishna and Ramana Maharshi.

– D.M.

5 ❦ *Renounce & Rejoice*

ARJUNA

¹O Krishna, you have recommended both the path of
selfless action and *sannyasa,* the path of renunciation
of action. Tell me definitely which is better.

KRISHNA

²Both renunciation of action and the selfless
performance of action lead to the supreme goal.
But the path of action is better than renunciation.

³Those who have attained perfect renunciation are
free from any sense of duality; they are unaffected
by likes and dislikes, Arjuna, and are free from
the bondage of self-will. ⁴The immature think that
knowledge and action are different, but the wise see
them as the same. The person who is established
in one path will attain the rewards of both. ⁵The
goal of knowledge and the goal of service are
the same; those who fail to see this are blind.

⁶Perfect renunciation is difficult to attain without
performing action. But the wise, following the
path of selfless service, quickly reach Brahman.

⁷Those who follow the path of service, who have
completely purified themselves and conquered their
senses and self-will, see the Self in all creatures
and are untouched by any action they perform.

⁸Those who know this truth, whose consciousness
is unified, think always, "I am not the doer." While
seeing or hearing, touching or smelling; eating,
moving about, or sleeping; breathing ⁹or speaking,
letting go or holding on, even opening or closing
the eyes, they understand that these are only the
movements of the senses among sense objects.

¹⁰Those who surrender to Brahman all selfish
attachments are like the leaf of a lotus floating
clean and dry in water. Sin cannot touch them.
¹¹Renouncing their selfish attachments, those who
follow the path of service work with body, senses,
and mind for the sake of self-purification.

¹²Those whose consciousness is unified abandon
all attachment to the results of action and attain

supreme peace. But those whose desires are
fragmented, who are selfishly attached to the results
of their work, are bound in everything they do.

¹³Those who renounce attachment in all their
deeds live content in the "city of nine gates,"
the body, as its master. They are not driven to
act, nor do they involve others in action.

¹⁴Neither the sense of acting, nor actions, nor the
connection of cause and effect comes from the
Lord of this world. These three arise from nature.

¹⁵The Lord does not partake in the good and evil
deeds of any person; judgment is clouded when
wisdom is obscured by ignorance. ¹⁶But ignorance
is destroyed by knowledge of the Self within.
The light of this knowledge shines like the sun,
revealing the supreme Brahman. ¹⁷Those who cast
off sin through this knowledge, absorbed in the
Lord and established in him as their one goal and
refuge, are not reborn as separate creatures.

¹⁸Those who possess this wisdom have equal
regard for all. They see the same Self in a spiritual
aspirant and an outcaste, in an elephant, a cow, and

a dog. [19]Such people have mastered life. With even mind they rest in Brahman, who is perfect and is everywhere the same. [20]They are not elated by good fortune nor depressed by bad. With mind established in Brahman, they are free from delusion. [21]Not dependent on any external support, they realize the joy of spiritual awareness. With consciousness unified through meditation, they live in abiding joy.

[22]Pleasures conceived in the world of the senses have a beginning and an end and give birth to misery, Arjuna. The wise do not look for happiness in them. [23]But those who overcome the impulses of lust and anger which arise in the body are made whole and live in joy. [24]They find their joy, their rest, and their light completely within themselves. United with the Lord, they attain nirvana in Brahman.

[25]Healed of their sins and conflicts, working for the good of all beings, the holy sages attain nirvana in Brahman. [26]Free from anger and selfish desire, unified in mind, those who follow the path of yoga and realize the Self are established forever in that supreme state.

[27]Closing their eyes, steadying their breathing, and focusing their attention on the center of spiritual

consciousness, [28]the wise master their senses, mind, and intellect through meditation. Self-realization is their only goal. Freed from selfish desire, fear, and anger, they live in freedom always. [29]Knowing me as the friend of all creatures, the Lord of the universe, the end of all offerings and all spiritual disciplines, they attain eternal peace.

▯: *The Practice of Meditation*

THIS IS SURELY one of the most intriguing chapters of the Gita, for here we are given a detailed explanation of meditation addressed to the layperson. The same meditation techniques are given in more esoteric writings, such as the *Yoga Sutras* of Patanjali, but the Gita does it more simply, without any unnecessary mystery or complexity.

This chapter also explores the question, "Who is the true yogi?" This word *yogi* may bring to mind images of amazing people who do strange contortions with their bodies. Yogis are still thought of as standing on their heads or reclining on a bed of nails. It is true that there are many practitioners of a kind of yoga that involves physical exercises and postures; and there are those who have achieved remarkable feats like lying on beds of nails, or even being buried alive and surviving. But this physical side of yoga (called *hatha yoga,* "the yoga of force") is not what is meant in the Gita. In fact, though physical techniques have a place, the Gita regards undue emphasis on them as outside the normal course of spiritual development.

In the Gita, the word *yogi* often has a more modest definition: it can mean a person who does his or her job with detachment from the rewards (6:1), or it can be rendered as "one who has attained the goal of meditation." For *yogi* literally means "one who is accomplished in yoga," and *yoga* means "integration of the spirit." In this sense, *yoga* means wholeness or the process of becoming whole at the deepest spiritual level. The word *yoga* is also often used as a synonym for *raja yoga,* the practice of meditation as taught by Patanjali; for meditation is the direct means of becoming integrated, united with one's truest, deepest Self. Thus a yogi, among other things, is a person who is an adept at meditation.

Until now, Krishna has been instructing Arjuna in the need for karma yoga, the active life of service. Now Krishna is ready to initiate him into the practice of the more interior disciplines of the spiritual life. Karma yoga, he says, is the path for those who wish to climb the mountain of Self-realization; for those who have reached the summit, the path is *shama,* the peace of contemplation. At the beginning of the spiritual life, great exertion is required; as the summit is approached, though the climb gets no easier, the dimension of contemplation or stillness is added. Many spiritual traditions, of course, use this image when speaking of the religious quest. The mountaintop is the place where the holy, like Moses, commune with God; and St. John of the Cross speaks of climbing the mountain of Carmel.

In climbing this mountain, willpower, self-help, and intense personal effort are absolute essentials. The literal translation of verse 5 is "one should lift oneself up by one's Self" – a play on the word *atman,* which can mean the highest Self as well as self in the ordinary sense. One's self is thus one's friend or one's own enemy. The "lower self" is self-will – will in the negative, selfish sense. An unruly will twisted toward self-aggrandizement is an enemy lurking right inside the fort, where it can do the most damage. But those who "have conquered themselves by themselves" have their truest friend in the Self. Only those who have genuine self-discipline, who are "self-conquered," live in peace.

These, Krishna says, are true yogis. They cannot harbor any malice, cannot even bring themselves to look upon anyone as an enemy. They are *samabuddhi,* "of equable mind." The true yogis, who are fully integrated on all levels of consciousness, feel everyone's joy and sorrow just as if it were their own. They see the Self in all beings, everywhere.

How is this self-conquest to be made? Very simply, the Gita teaches that the mind must be made one-pointed through the practice of meditation. This is the basic technique. In the Gita we do not see the tendency for elaboration, for ritual and mystery, that we sometimes find in the Hindu tradition. Krishna simply tells Arjuna, first, that he must find an appropriate place to meditate. A suitable spot for his practice will be clean and comfortable. In a nod to tradition, one verse recommends the meditation seat be covered with kusha grass and a deerskin – the traditional seat of the yogi. The important thing, however, is not how the meditation seat is made, but what is going on in the mind. Meditation is an internal discipline to make the mind one-pointed, absolutely concentrated.

Second, Krishna instructs Arjuna to hold the body, head, and neck in a straight line. This may seem esoteric – a reference to the contortion-school of yoga – but it has a practical purpose. Sitting absolutely straight, with the spinal column erect, prevents drowsiness. Also, in advanced stages of meditation, it allows for the free flow of vital energy or *kundalini* (see glossary).

Then practical advice is given: moderation is the path. Neither extreme asceticism nor indulgence will aid meditation. An initial acquaintance with Hindu culture may give the impression that it fosters either the sensuality of the *Kama Sutra* or the asceticism of the hermit. It is true that in Indian civilization we can easily see the development of the sensual and artistic in many manifestations – in painting, sculpture, music, and dance. And Indian cuisine is famous for its variety of flavors and spices. India also presents us with the austere simplicity of the wandering holy man or *sadhu*. The Gita, however, recommends the middle path. Success in meditation, Krishna says, comes neither to those who eat or sleep too much nor to those who eat or sleep too little. The body should be neither overindulged nor treated harshly – the same recommendation the Buddha offers.

This chapter contains the famous verse (6:19) comparing the mind to a steady flame. By its very nature the untrained mind is restless, constantly wandering here and there trying to fulfill its desires. It flickers wildly like a flame in a storm – never blown completely out, yet at the mercy of the wind. Wherever the mind wanders, Krishna says, it must be brought back to its source; it must learn to rest in the Self. Once it is at home in the depths of contemplation, the mind becomes steady, like an upright, unflickering flame in a windless place. In this deep meditation, and only there, can the human being find true fulfillment. Then "the still mind touches Brahman and enjoys bliss."

Now Arjuna asks an inevitable question. Krishna is far ahead of him, and the struggling disciple simply can't catch up. He says, "My mind is so restless and unsteady that I cannot even comprehend anything about this state of mystic peace you are talking about." The mind is so powerful, so turbulent, that trying to bring it under control is like trying to catch the wind.

Krishna admits that the mind is terribly hard to train, but

he maintains that it can be done through regular practice if one has detachment. It is interesting that he does not offer to help Arjuna here; that will come later. For now, he tells Arjuna that he must do it for himself, through hard work and detachment from private, personal motives.

Then Arjuna asks a rather surprising question: what happens to the person who believes in a spiritual goal but does not pursue it to the end? What if one of his more powerful compulsive desires gets the better of him, scattering his resolution the way a cloud is scattered by the wind? Either Arjuna is not prepared to seek Self-realization or he is afraid that somehow he might fail if he tried. If he were to fail, he asks, would he have lost everything – all that he had given up in worldly life as well as his goal of self-fulfillment?

Affectionately, Krishna assures Arjuna that no attempt to improve his spiritual condition could be a wasted effort. Even looking ahead to the next life, he has nothing to lose and everything to gain. He will be reborn in a household suitable for taking up his quest where he left off. In his next life, he will feel drawn to the spiritual goal once again, and he will have a head start.

– D.M.

6 ॥ *The Practice of Meditation*

KRISHNA

[1]It is not those who lack energy or refrain from action, but those who work without expectation of reward who attain the goal of meditation. Theirs is true renunciation. [2]Therefore, Arjuna, you should understand that renunciation and the performance of selfless service are the same. Those who cannot renounce attachment to the results of their work are far from the path.

[3]For aspirants who want to climb the mountain of spiritual awareness, the path is selfless work; for those who have ascended to yoga the path is stillness and peace. [4]When you have freed yourself from attachment to the results of work, and from desires for the enjoyment of sense objects, you will ascend to the unitive state.

⁵Reshape yourself through the power of your
will; never let yourself be degraded by self-
will. The will is the only friend of the Self,
and the will is the only enemy of the Self.

⁶To those who have conquered themselves,
the will is a friend. But it is the enemy of those
who have not found the Self within them.

⁷The supreme Reality stands revealed in the
consciousness of those who have conquered
themselves. They live in peace, alike in cold and
heat, pleasure and pain, praise and blame.

⁸They are completely fulfilled by spiritual wisdom and
Self-realization. Having conquered their senses, they
have climbed to the summit of human consciousness.
To such people a clod of dirt, a stone, and gold are
the same. ⁹They are equally disposed to family,
enemies, and friends, to those who support them and
those who are hostile, to the good and the evil alike.
Because they are impartial, they rise to great heights.

¹⁰Those who aspire to the state of yoga should seek
the Self in inner solitude through meditation. With
body and mind controlled they should constantly

practice one-pointedness, free from expectations
and attachment to material possessions.

[11]Select a clean spot, neither too high nor too low,
and seat yourself firmly on a cloth, a deerskin, and
kusha grass. [12]Then, once seated, strive to still your
thoughts. Make your mind one-pointed in meditation,
and your heart will be purified. [13]Hold your body,
head, and neck firmly in a straight line, and keep
your eyes from wandering. [14]With all fears dissolved
in the peace of the Self and all actions dedicated to
Brahman, controlling the mind and fixing it on me, sit
in meditation with me as your only goal. [15]With senses
and mind constantly controlled through meditation,
united with the Self within, an aspirant attains
nirvana, the state of abiding joy and peace in me.

[16]Arjuna, those who eat too much or eat too little,
who sleep too much or sleep too little, will not
succeed in meditation. [17]But those who are temperate
in eating and sleeping, work and recreation, will
come to the end of sorrow through meditation.
[18]Through constant effort they learn to withdraw
the mind from selfish cravings and absorb it in
the Self. Thus they attain the state of union.

¹⁹When meditation is mastered, the mind is unwavering like the flame of a lamp in a windless place. ²⁰In the still mind, in the depths of meditation, the Self reveals itself. Beholding the Self by means of the Self, an aspirant knows the joy and peace of complete fulfillment. ²¹Having attained that abiding joy beyond the senses, revealed in the stilled mind, they never swerve from the eternal truth. ²²They desire nothing else and cannot be shaken by the heaviest burden of sorrow.

²³The practice of meditation frees one from all affliction. This is the path of yoga. Follow it with determination and sustained enthusiasm. ²⁴Renouncing wholeheartedly all selfish desires and expectations, use your will to control the senses. ²⁵Little by little, through patience and repeated effort, the mind will become stilled in the Self.

²⁶Wherever the mind wanders, restless and diffuse in its search for satisfaction without, lead it within; train it to rest in the Self. ²⁷Abiding joy comes to those who still the mind. Freeing themselves from the taint of self-will, with their consciousness unified, they become one with Brahman.

[28]The infinite joy of touching Brahman is easily attained by those who are free from the burden of evil and established within themselves. [29]They see the Self in every creature and all creation in the Self. With consciousness unified through meditation, they see everything with an equal eye.

[30]I am ever present to those who have realized me in every creature. Seeing all life as my manifestation, they are never separated from me. [31]They worship me in the hearts of all, and all their actions proceed from me. Wherever they may live, they abide in me.

[32]When a person responds to the joys and sorrows of others as if they were his own, he has attained the highest state of spiritual union.

ARJUNA

[33]O Krishna, the stillness of divine union which you describe is beyond my comprehension. How can the mind, which is so restless, attain lasting peace? [34]Krishna, the mind is restless, turbulent, powerful, violent; trying to control it is like trying to tame the wind.

KRISHNA

³⁵It is true that the mind is restless and difficult to control. But it can be conquered, Arjuna, through regular practice and detachment. ³⁶Those who lack self-control will find it difficult to progress in meditation; but those who are self-controlled, striving earnestly through the right means, will attain the goal.

ARJUNA

³⁷Krishna, what happens to one who has faith but who lacks self-control and wanders from the path, not attaining success in yoga? ³⁸If he becomes deluded on the spiritual path, will he lose the support of both worlds, like a cloud scattered in the sky? ³⁹Krishna, you can dispel all doubts; remove this doubt which binds me.

KRISHNA

⁴⁰Arjuna, my son, such a person will not be destroyed. No one who does good work will ever come to a bad end, either here or in the world to come.

⁴¹When such people die, they go to other realms where the righteous live. They dwell there for countless years and then are reborn ⁴²into a home

which is pure and prosperous. Or they may be born
into a family where meditation is practiced; to be
born into such a family is extremely rare. ⁴³The
wisdom they have acquired in previous lives will be
reawakened, Arjuna, and they will strive even harder
for Self-realization. ⁴⁴Indeed, they will be driven
on by the strength of their past disciplines. Even
one who inquires after the practice of meditation
rises above those who simply perform rituals.

⁴⁵Through constant effort over many lifetimes,
a person becomes purified of all selfish desires
and attains the supreme goal of life.

⁴⁶Meditation is superior to severe asceticism and the
path of knowledge. It is also superior to selfless service.
May you attain the goal of meditation, Arjuna! ⁴⁷Even
among those who meditate, that man or woman who
worships me with perfect faith, completely absorbed
in me, is the most firmly established in yoga.

◉: *Wisdom from Realization*

IN SANSKRIT THIS chapter is called "The Yoga of Wisdom and Realization" – or "The Yoga of Wisdom from Realization." The term used for wisdom is *jnana*; for realization, *vijnana*. There is room for confusion in this terminology, as *jnana* and *vijnana* are open to differing interpretations. Both words are from the root *jna*, "to know," which is related to the Greek word *gnosis*. The prefix *vi* added to a noun usually intensifies its meaning; so *vijnana* could mean to know intensely or to a greater degree. In this context, however, *jnana* is the standard term for the highest kind of knowledge: not scholarship or book-learning but direct knowledge of God, spiritual wisdom. If we take *jnana* in this sense, we are not left with an obvious meaning for *vijnana*, a "more intense kind of jnana." Ramakrishna takes *vijnana* to mean an intimate, practical familiarity with God, the ability to carry through in daily affairs with the more abstract understanding that is *jnana*. Ramakrishna says, "One who has merely heard of fire has *ajnana*, ignorance. One who has seen fire has *jnana*. But one who has actually built a fire and cooked on it has *vijnana*."

In this chapter we find ourselves following several trails and sometimes lose the unifying theme, which is knowledge of the supreme reality underlying nature. Eventually, however, we come back to the starting point: knowledge contrasted with ignorance, transcendent reality as opposed to the phenomenal world.

But to pursue the byways. First, Krishna's "two natures" are discussed. On the one hand, he has created out of himself the elements and all things that make up the phenomenal world. Beyond this is Krishna's spiritual nature as the transcendent Lord of the universe. Here the Gita is referring to a concept that later became a basis of the Sankhya school of Hindu philosophy. Sankhya recognized two fundamental principles underlying all things: prakriti, the principle of mind and matter, and Purusha, the principle of pure spirit. The union of these two eternal, fundamental forces sets in motion the creation of the world as we know it. Their union also shapes and defines all ordinary human experience. In Sankhya, the goal of Self-realization is seen as the final freeing of the spirit (Purusha) from its flirtation with mind and matter (prakriti).

Unlike Sankhya, however, in the Gita it is Krishna who is behind both prakriti and Purusha. In this chapter, Krishna is presented as the Creator of the world. His divine nature can be glimpsed in his bewildering and wonderful creation. In much

Hindu mythology, it is the god Brahma who takes credit for creating the world. It is he, the four-faced deity, who has flung forth the manifold worlds of this and former (as well as future) universes. But in the mythology of Vishnu, Brahma is born in the lotus that grows from Vishnu's navel. The lotus is Vishnu's womb. In it Brahma is born, and at Vishnu's urging he creates the worlds. Vishnu is the real Creator; Brahma is a demi-god born of Vishnu's will to create. Here in the Gita Krishna directly assumes all the roles and honors usually shared with the other aspects of God worshipped in the Hindu faith. It is not that these other divine personifications are rejected, but simply that all attention is on Krishna. For the author of the Gita, Krishna is the form of God to be worshipped, and for the time being all other forms of God disappear. Krishna alone is. In fact, one verse states that whatever other god one seems to worship, one is in reality approaching Krishna himself. Worshipping him, knowing him, enables the devotee to attain the goal.

Though the word is not used in the Gita, the idea of the world as Krishna's *lila*, his play, became a cherished theme of later Hinduism. Krishna, it is said, created the world in play: just as a child might desire to have companions to play with, Krishna desired companions, and made the world. Krishna participates in the game of life; his divine qualities shine through in the world wherever there is excellence of any kind. He is, he tells Arjuna, the essence of every created thing: the sapidity of water, the brightness of fire, the effort of the spiritual aspirant. This may be what is meant by the *vijnana* of our title – the mystic's vision of the divine as present here and now is perhaps the real meaning of the term.

The word *maya* appears here, though not for the first time in the Gita. Just as the concepts of prakriti and Purusha are later developed in Sankhya philosophy, *maya* is later built into the formal structure of Vedanta, another of the six major schools of Indian philosophy. The word *maya* comes from the root *ma*, "to measure out," and originally meant the power of a deity to create, especially to create what Indian philosophy calls "name and form": matter and its percepts. Maya was the magical capacity to create form and illusion – a god's divine power to put on a disguise, or to fling forth world after world of life. Maya is also the outward look of things, the passing show that conceals immortal being. Maya can be both delightful and dangerous, alluring and yet treacherous. The gunas, the three basic qualities of all created things, swirl within the world of maya. Crossing over the ocean of maya is the goal of the wise voyager, and one boat is devotion. In this chapter the Gita begins to stress the importance of love and devotion – themes that later become dominant.

Krishna's true nature is hidden by maya (7:25). The dangers of maya are not depicted strongly in this chapter, but the "delusions" – *moha* – of life in maya's world are hinted at; they are, essentially, the self-centered attachments Krishna has been warning against. *Moha,* which means confusion or delusion, is something like dreaming while awake, "living in a dream." The duality of attachment and aversion (love and hate) beguiles the mind into this *moha*-swoon right at birth (7:27). Knowing Krishna, and devotion to him, is the way beyond this delusion. Thus chapter 7 contrasts wisdom (*jnana* and *vijnana*) with the delusion (*moha*) of spiritual ignorance.

We find here many seminal ideas that are elaborated in the later philosophies of Sankhya and Vedanta. These concepts of prakriti, Purusha, and maya do not originate with the Gita, however. The word *maya* appears in the Rig Veda, the most ancient of the Vedas, and Purusha is a recurring theme in the Upanishads. The Gita is a halfway point between the spontaneous insights of the Upanishads and the later, highly formalized philosophical systems. In the Gita we find an organized presentation of these and other key concepts without a cumbersome technical explanation.

— D.M.

7 ◉ *Wisdom from Realization*

KRISHNA

¹With your mind intent on me, Arjuna,
discipline yourself with the practice of yoga.
Depend on me completely. Listen, and I
will dispel all your doubts; you will come to
know me fully and be united with me.

²I will give you both jnana and vijnana.
When both these are realized, there is
nothing more you need to know.

³One person in many thousands may seek perfection,
yet of these only a few reach the goal and come to
realize me. ⁴Earth, water, fire, air, *akasha,* mind,
intellect, and ego – these are the eight divisions
of my prakriti. ⁵But beyond this I have another,
higher nature, Arjuna; it supports the whole
universe and is the source of life in all beings.

⁶In these two aspects of my nature is the womb of all creation. The birth and dissolution of the cosmos itself take place in me. ⁷There is nothing that exists separate from me, Arjuna. The entire universe is suspended from me as my necklace of jewels.

⁸Arjuna, I am the taste of pure water and the radiance of the sun and moon. I am the sacred word and the sound heard in air, and the courage of human beings. ⁹I am the sweet fragrance in the earth and the radiance of fire; I am the life in every creature and the striving of the spiritual aspirant.

¹⁰My eternal seed, Arjuna, is to be found in every creature. I am the power of discrimination in those who are intelligent, and the glory of the noble. ¹¹In those who are strong, I am strength, free from passion and selfish attachment. I am desire itself, if that desire is in harmony with the purpose of life.

¹²The states of sattva, rajas, and tamas come from me, but I am not in them. ¹³These three gunas deceive the world: people fail to look beyond them to me, supreme and imperishable. ¹⁴The three gunas make up my divine maya, difficult to overcome. But they cross over

this maya who take refuge in me. ¹⁵Others are deluded by maya; performing evil deeds, they have no devotion to me. Having lost all discrimination, they follow the way of their lower nature.

¹⁶Good people come to worship me for different reasons. Some come to the spiritual life because of suffering, some in order to understand life; some come through a desire to achieve life's purpose, and some come who are men and women of wisdom. ¹⁷Unwavering in devotion, always united with me, the man or woman of wisdom surpasses all the others. To them I am the dearest beloved, and they are very dear to me. ¹⁸All those who follow the spiritual path are blessed. But the wise who are always established in union, for whom there is no higher goal than me, may be regarded as my very Self.

¹⁹After many births the wise seek refuge in me, seeing me everywhere and in everything. Such great souls are very rare. ²⁰There are others whose discrimination is misled by many desires. Following their own nature, they worship lower gods, practicing various rites.

²¹When a person is devoted to something with complete faith, I unify his faith in that. ²²Then, when

faith is completely unified, one gains the object of devotion. In this way, every desire is fulfilled by me. ²³Those whose understanding is small attain only transient satisfaction: those who worship the gods go to the gods. But my devotees come to me.

²⁴Through lack of understanding, people believe that I, the Unmanifest, have entered into some form. They fail to realize my true nature, which transcends birth and death. ²⁵Few see through the veil of maya. The world, deluded, does not know that I am without birth and changeless. ²⁶I know everything about the past, the present, and the future, Arjuna; but there is no one who knows me completely.

²⁷Delusion arises from the duality of attraction and aversion, Arjuna; every creature is deluded by these from birth. ²⁸But those who have freed themselves from all wrongdoing are firmly established in worship of me. Their actions are pure, and they are free from the delusion caused by the pairs of opposites.

²⁹Those who take refuge in me, striving for liberation from old age and death, come to know Brahman, the Self, and the nature of all action. ³⁰Those who see me ruling the cosmos, who see me in

the *adhibhuta,* the *adhidaiva,* and the *adhiyajna,*
are conscious of me even at the time of death.

8: *The Eternal Godhead*

THIS CHAPTER ALLUDES briefly to several important concepts presented more fully in the Upanishads, and it will be helpful to quote the Upanishads to elucidate these points. Also, this chapter presents a very ancient view of the soul's journey after death. These ideas about the afterlife did not originate in the Gita, and are even more ancient than the Upanishads. Another ancient concept here is that of a cyclical universe, which is elaborated in other Hindu scriptures in great detail; this chapter merely refers to it in passing.

The chapter begins with Arjuna asking what appear to be questions of theology, but the role of theologian does not fit him naturally. These questions are asked in response to the technical terms mentioned in the last verse of chapter 7. The sense of Krishna's answer is in accord with what he said earlier about his maya: he is God immanent in all things as well as God transcendent.

But it is Arjuna's other question that determines the direction the discourse now takes. Arjuna asks how Krishna can be known at the hour of death. Here, of course, Arjuna means Krishna in his cosmic, mystical aspect, so he is asking in essence, "How can the Self-realized person enter the supreme state of immortality at the time of death?" Krishna replies that whoever remembers him at the time of death will enter *madbhavam,* "my being." If Arjuna can remember Krishna in the hour of death, he will be united with Krishna and enter into immortality.

In fact, whatever it may be, the content of the mind at the hour of death directs the soul in its journey to rebirth. Thus the mind influences the evolution of the soul as it moves into the next life. Whatever a person thinks about in life – his or her deepest motivations – are likely to be the last thoughts at the time of death. So there is a continuity between this life and the next, and all the baggage of desire and motivation goes right along with the soul. But here Krishna is talking about the person – he hopes Arjuna will be such a one – who has no worldly baggage, who will remember Krishna at the final hour.

To ensure he will focus his devotion on Krishna at the hour of death, Arjuna should make a practice of remembering him continually now. If he makes his mind one-pointed in meditation and learns to focus his being on Krishna, then naturally at the time of death he will think of nothing else. Otherwise, in the chaos of death, he will panic and lose his way.

Krishna describes in detail what happens to consciousness at the moment of death (8:12–13). These verses actually describe the yogis as being in control of the process of death. Directing their consciousness step by step through the difficult ordeal of leaving the body, they attain the supreme goal. This idea is also accepted by one of the greatest teachers of meditation in ancient India, Patanjali, who says in the *Yoga Sutras* that the yogi dies at will. Similar descriptions of the death process occur in the Upanishads, though there the dying person is not necessarily in control. The Upanishads give a detailed account:

> When the Self seems to become weak and sink into unconsciousness, the vital breaths gather to him. Then he takes with him those particles of light and descends into the heart. When the consciousness that is in the eye turns back, the dying person no longer sees any form. "He is becoming one," they say; "he does not see." "He is becoming one," they say; "he does not smell." "He is becoming one," they say; "he does not taste." "He is becoming one," they say; "he does not speak." "He is becoming one," they say; "he does not hear." "He is becoming one," they say; "he does not think or touch or know." The point of his heart lights up, and by that light the Self departs, either through the eye, or the skull, or through some other door of the body. And when he departs,

life departs: and when life departs, all other vital forces depart after it. He is conscious, and with consciousness he leaves the body. Then his knowledge and his works and his previous impressions go along with him. (Brihadaranyaka Upanishad IV.4.1–2)

First consciousness is withdrawn from the senses. The dying no longer hear or see what is going on around them. They are still conscious, but the "light" of consciousness has been withdrawn from the senses, here called the "gates" of the body. There are said to be nine such gates: two eyes, two nostrils, two ears, the mouth, and the organs of generation and excretion. Sometimes two more are added: the navel and the sagittal suture, located at the top of the skull and called in Sanskrit *brahmarandhra,* "the aperture of Brahman."

When consciousness has been withdrawn from these gates, Krishna says, "the mind is placed ['locked up'] in the heart." (8:12) Here, as in Christian mysticism, it is the heart and not the head that is taken to be the home of the soul. Probably what is meant is the heart *chakra,* the center of consciousness corresponding to the center of the chest. *Prana* (vital energy) and awareness have been withdrawn from the outer frontiers of personality and consolidated within. At this stage of the death process an ordinary person has no access to the will; but it is just here that prana, with conscious awareness, must be made to move upwards to the head. If prana leaves the body through the brahmarandhra, there will be no rebirth: that is, the dying person will enter samadhi at the time of death. In samadhi, prana is withdrawn from lower levels of awareness to rush upwards to the seventh center at the crown of the head. This is possible only for the yogi who has thoroughly mastered meditation and the control of prana. If prana exits through some other one of the eleven doors of the body, the Upanishads say, the state of immortality will not be gained:

> When he departs from this body, he ascends with the rays of the sun, repeating the syllable *Om*. As soon as he thinks of it, he comes to the sun. That, indeed, is the door to the next world. Those who know enter; those who do not know are stopped. There is a verse:
>
> *A hundred and one subtle tracks lead from the heart;*
> *One of these goes upwards to the crown of the head.*
> *Going up by it, he goes to eternal life.*
> *Others depart in various directions.*
> (Chandogya Upanishad VIII.6.5–6)

In the Gita, as well as in this passage from the Chandogya Upanishad, the mantram *Om* is used. If the yogis can remember the mantram even as consciousness itself is departing the body – and, the Gita adds, if they can meditate on Krishna – they will go to the "highest goal." Relinquishing the body in a state of samadhi, they attain the mystic eternity that is union with Krishna.

In this chapter the Gita alludes to the two paths, "northern" and "southern," that the soul may take after death. Verses 24–25 present in abbreviated form what the Brihadaranyaka Upanishad spells out in obscure detail:

> Those who know this, who meditate upon Truth with faith while living in the forest, go to the light, from light to day, from day to the fortnight of the moon's waxing, from the waxing fortnight to the six months of the sun's northern journey, from those six months to the world of the devas, from the world of the devas to the sun, from the sun to the lightning. Then a spirit approaches them and leads them to the world of Brahman. In that world they live for eternal ages. They do not return again.
>
> But those who conquer worlds through sacrifice, charity, and austerity pass into the smoke, from the smoke into the night, from the night into the fortnight of the waning moon, from the fortnight of the waning moon into the six months of the sun's southern journey, from there into the world of the ancestors, from the world of the ancestors into the moon, . . . and from there to rebirth. (Brihadaranyaka Upanishad VI.2.15–16)

"Northern and southern paths" refers to the path of the sun, which seems to move northward after the winter solstice and southward after the summer solstice. To die during the period in which the sun is moving southward was considered inauspicious; dying during the period after the winter solstice, when the sun is moving back north, meant the soul might take the northern path which leads to immortality. In the Gita and the Upanishads, this "northern path" has come to signify that the soul has been released from karma and need not be reborn. The southern path, by contrast, leads the soul to a new birth in this world, a birth suitable to its karma. This view of the soul's journey after death has a primordial quality about it, giving the feeling that it far predates even the Upanishads. Perhaps it is a belief of very ancient times that found its way into the Upanishads, which say that the spiritually ready soul makes the journey of the northern route while those who have only practiced rituals take the southern.

This chapter also briefly alludes to the Days and Nights of Brahma. Brahma is the Creator of the Hindu trinity, who brings forth the cosmos at the will of Vishnu. But Brahma in a sense is not in control of this creative process. Just as day follows night in eternal, unvarying rhythm, so does the entire universe undergo cycles of creation, death, and new birth. As the Day of Brahma dawns, the cosmos comes into being; as the Day comes to an end, the entire creation dies and ceases to exist. Then, for a Night as long as the cosmic Day, the universe rests. It ceases to be – or, rather, it continues only in a subtle, unmanifest form, a dream in the mind of Vishnu, who lies sleeping on the waves of the cosmic ocean. Then, without deviating from the eternal rhythm, the cosmos is reborn when the Night is over. The new universe dawns, and Brahma once again moves into his active, creative Day.

Scholars have noted that this grand vision of the cosmos being born, dying, and being reborn for eternity – cosmos after cosmos arising from the black immensity of nothingness – is quite similar to modern theories of the expanding and contracting universe put forward by contemporary cosmology. The vast time spans accepted by present-day physics are also similar to the cosmic Days and Nights of Brahma. Each Day lasts for a thousand yugas, which equals 4,320,000,000 years. For this near-eternity of time the universe lives and grows; then it dies and lies dormant for an equal time, before the new Day dawns.

There is a state of being, however, that is higher than the perishable cosmos, which is not born and does not die the cosmic death. Here (8:20) it is called simply *avyakta*, the Unmanifest. This is the supreme goal of all living things, and it is Krishna's home (8:21). Returning to this final resting place, the soul enters into immortal bliss and is not reborn.

– D.M.

8 ॥ *The Eternal Godhead*

ARJUNA

[1]O Krishna, what is Brahman, and what is the nature
of action? What is the *adhyatma,* the *adhibhuta,*
the *adhidaiva*? [2]What is the *adhiyajna,* the supreme
sacrifice, and how is it to be offered? How are the
self-controlled united with you at the time of death?

KRISHNA

[3]My highest nature, the imperishable Brahman,
gives every creature its existence and lives in
every creature as the adhyatma. My action is
creation and the bringing forth of creatures. [4]The
adhibhuta is the perishable body; the adhidaiva is
Purusha, eternal spirit. The adhiyajna, the supreme
sacrifice, is made to me as the Lord within you.

[5]Those who remember me at the time of death
will come to me. Do not doubt this. [6]Whatever
occupies the mind at the time of death determines

the destination of the dying; always they will
tend toward that state of being. ⁷Therefore,
remember me at all times and fight on. With your
heart and mind intent on me, you will surely
come to me. ⁸When you make your mind one-
pointed through regular practice of meditation,
you will find the supreme glory of the Lord.

⁹The Lord is the supreme poet, the first cause, the
sovereign ruler, subtler than the tiniest particle,
the support of all, inconceivable, bright as the
sun, beyond darkness. ¹⁰Remembering him in
this way at the time of death, through devotion
and the power of meditation, with your mind
completely stilled and your concentration fixed
in the center of spiritual awareness between the
eyebrows, you will realize the supreme Lord.

¹¹I will tell you briefly of the eternal state all
scriptures affirm, which can be entered only
by those who are self-controlled and free from
selfish passions. Those whose lives are dedicated
to Brahman attain this supreme goal.

¹²Remembering me at the time of death, close
down the doors of the senses and place the mind

in the heart. Then, while absorbed in meditation, focus all energy upwards to the head. ¹³Repeating in this state the divine name, the syllable *Om* that represents the changeless Brahman, you will go forth from the body and attain the supreme goal.

¹⁴I am easily attained by the person who always remembers me and is attached to nothing else. Such a person is a true yogi, Arjuna. ¹⁵Great souls make their lives perfect and discover me; they are freed from mortality and the suffering of this separate existence. ¹⁶Every creature in the universe is subject to rebirth, Arjuna, except the one who is united with me.

¹⁷Those who understand the cosmic laws know that the Day of Brahma ends after a thousand yugas and the Night of Brahma ends after a thousand yugas. ¹⁸When the day of Brahma dawns, forms are brought forth from the Unmanifest; when the night of Brahma comes, these forms merge in the Formless again. ¹⁹This multitude of beings is created and destroyed again and again in the succeeding days and nights of Brahma. ²⁰But beyond this formless state there is another, unmanifested reality, which is eternal and is not dissolved when the cosmos is destroyed. ²¹Those who realize life's supreme goal know that

I am unmanifested and unchanging. Having come home to me, they never return to separate existence.

²²This supreme Lord who pervades all existence, the true Self of all creatures, may be realized through undivided love. ²³There are two paths, Arjuna, which the soul may follow at the time of death. One leads to rebirth and the other to liberation.

²⁴The six months of the northern path of the sun, the path of light, of fire, of day, of the bright fortnight, leads knowers of Brahman to the supreme goal. ²⁵The six months of the southern path of the sun, the path of smoke, of night, of the dark fortnight, leads other souls to the light of the moon and to rebirth.

²⁶These two paths, the light and the dark, are said to be eternal, leading some to liberation and others to rebirth. ²⁷Once you have known these two paths, Arjuna, you can never be deluded again. Attain this knowledge through perseverance in yoga. ²⁸There is merit in studying the scriptures, in selfless service, austerity, and giving, but the practice of meditation carries you beyond all these to the supreme abode of the highest Lord.

◻: *The Royal Path*

THIS CHAPTER PRAISES Krishna as the Supreme Being who has created the world and dwells immanent in his creation. Krishna's exalted nature is stressed, and warning is given to those who think that God is limited to his creation. It is true that Krishna has taken on a human form, but those who see only a limited human being and show him disrespect are courting great spiritual harm. These verses contain a warning for those who would underestimate Krishna's divine power.

In this chapter Krishna replaces the many gods and goddesses of the usual Hindu pantheon, each of which represents a different divine power; here Krishna is seen as containing within himself all such powers. It is Krishna and Krishna alone who is to be worshipped: he is the goal, the support, the only refuge, the one true friend; he is the beginning and the end (9:18).

It follows that those who practice a ritual religion, offering the ritual sacrifices ordained by the Vedas, do not attain the true goal of their lives. True, they do enjoy heaven after death. But when their store of merit is used up, they are born again in order to have another chance at turning away from personal gain and aiming at life's supreme goal. So long as they are motivated only by self-centered desires they must be born again and again, and their spiritual evolution either stands still or they make very little progress.

Even these souls, however, are really worshipping Krishna, though they do not know it. They seek Krishna, the Supreme Being, in all their wanderings through many, many lives and even in their sojourns in heaven, where they enjoy the reward of their good deeds. Because they do not know his real nature, however, they will not attain the goal, but will be reborn.

An endless round of rebirths may seem like a living damnation of the struggling soul – a harsh note that would be uncharacteristic of the Gita. But this is not a question of damnation. The purpose of life is to realize God, and until this is done, the soul cannot escape creating more karma which has to be worked out, however many lives it might take. The choice to turn toward Self-realization is always open.

The Gita does not dwell on the obstacles, however, but quickly goes on to reveal Krishna's more compassionate nature. It makes the point that whatever a person deeply desires – whatever he or she worships – will eventually be attained, in some life or other. In particular, to have real, selfless love, regardless of the object, is to love Krishna, the ultimate good. This kind of love, called *bhakti,* is far more potent than observances and rituals – a point the Gita is slowly revealing. But to have this devotion without understanding Krishna's nature is not enough. In the end, to attain his goal, Arjuna must have devotion and understand it is Krishna's universal aspect that he loves. Then he will truly attain the eternal, immortal state.

This chapter contains a famous and very popular series of verses:

> Whatever you do, make it an offering to me – the food you
> eat, the sacrifices you make, the help you give, even your
> suffering. In this way you will be freed from the bondage
> of karma, and from its results both pleasant and painful.
> (9:27–28)

Krishna accepts every offering made to him in the right spirit; he assures Arjuna of this. Then he demands that Arjuna make everything – every act, every meal, every sacrifice, every gift, even his sufferings – an offering to God. He demands this so that Arjuna can be released from the bondage of karma. This is a new emphasis, a new way. If Arjuna can live in complete union with Krishna's will, doing everything for Krishna alone, then by that very purity of will he will be free from selfish motives and thus released from karma. His spirit will be free, and he will attain his goal of mystic union with Krishna.

Krishna declares that he is impartial to all creatures: he neither favors nor rejects anyone. It is their sincere love that is important. Those who are truly devoted to Krishna live in him, and he abides in them. With some daring, probably at the risk of discomfort to the more orthodox, Krishna adds that even a sinner who takes wholehearted refuge in him becomes good. The word used is *sadhu,* which literally means a good person but has come to signify one who leads the spiritual life, giving up all selfish desires to achieve the final goal. The word for sinner, *sudurachara,* should not be passed by either. *Su* is literally "good"; *dur* is "bad": thus "one whose conduct is *really* bad," as we might say "good and hot" to mean really hot.

Krishna promises that his devotees must attain peace at last. No one who has genuine love and devotion can perish. The meaning here is taken to be "perish" in a spiritual sense, come to spiritual harm. The message of this chapter is simple. It contains no philosophy and only a little theology. The one message is: anyone who has real love, love for the Lord of Love who is in all creatures, will in the end attain the goal. This is the royal secret that Krishna had promised to reveal.

– D.M.

9 ◗: *The Royal Path*

KRISHNA

¹Because of your faith, I shall tell you the most
profound of secrets: obtaining both jnana
and vijnana, you will be free from all evil.

²This royal knowledge, this royal secret, is the
greatest purifier. Righteous and imperishable, it is
a joy to practice and can be directly experienced.
³But those who have no faith in the supreme
law of life do not find me, Arjuna. They return
to the world, passing from death to death.

⁴I pervade the entire universe in my unmanifested
form. All creatures find their existence in me,
but I am not limited by them. ⁵Behold my divine
mystery! These creatures do not really dwell in me,
and though I bring them forth and support them,
I am not confined within them. ⁶They move in me
as the winds move in every direction in space.

⁷At the end of the eon these creatures return to
unmanifested matter; at the beginning of the next
cycle I send them forth again. ⁸Controlling my
prakriti, again and again I bring forth these myriad
forms and subject them to the laws of prakriti. ⁹None
of these actions binds me, Arjuna. I am unattached
to them, so they do not disturb my nature.

¹⁰Under my watchful eye the laws of nature take
their course. Thus is the world set in motion; thus
the animate and the inanimate are created.

¹¹The immature do not look beyond physical
appearances to see my true nature as the Lord of all
creation. ¹²The knowledge of such deluded people
is empty; their lives are fraught with disaster and
evil, and their work and hopes are all in vain.

¹³But truly great souls seek my divine nature.
They worship me with a one-pointed mind,
having realized that I am the eternal source of
all. ¹⁴Constantly striving, they make firm their
resolve and worship me without wavering. Full
of devotion, they sing of my divine glory.

¹⁵Others follow the path of jnana, spiritual
wisdom. They see that where there is One,
that One is me; where there are many, all
are me; they see my face everywhere.

¹⁶I am the ritual and the sacrifice; I am true medicine
and the mantram. I am the offering and the fire which
consumes it, and the one to whom it is offered.

¹⁷I am the father and mother of this universe, and its
grandfather too; I am its entire support. I am the sum
of all knowledge, the purifier, the syllable *Om*; I am
the sacred scriptures, the Rig, Yajur, and Sama Vedas.

¹⁸I am the goal of life, the Lord and support
of all, the inner witness, the abode of all. I am
the only refuge, the one true friend; I am the
beginning, the staying, and the end of creation;
I am the womb and the eternal seed.

¹⁹I am heat; I give and withhold the
rain. I am immortality and I am death;
I am what is and what is not.

²⁰Those who follow the rituals given in the
Vedas, who offer sacrifices and take soma, free

themselves from evil and attain the vast heaven
of the gods, where they enjoy celestial pleasures.
²¹When they have enjoyed these fully, their merit
is exhausted and they return to this land of death.
Thus observing Vedic rituals but caught in an
endless chain of desires, they come and go.

²²Those who worship me and meditate on
me constantly, without any other thought
– I will provide for all their needs.

²³Those who worship other gods with faith and
devotion also worship me, Arjuna, even if they do
not observe the usual forms. ²⁴I am the object of all
worship, its enjoyer and Lord. But those who fail to
realize my true nature must be reborn. ²⁵Those who
worship the devas will go to the realm of the devas;
those who worship their ancestors will be united with
them after death. Those who worship phantoms will
become phantoms; but my devotees will come to me.

²⁶Whatever I am offered in devotion with a pure heart
– a leaf, a flower, fruit, or water – I accept with joy.
²⁷Whatever you do, make it an offering to me – the
food you eat, the sacrifices you make, the help you
give, even your suffering. ²⁸In this way you will be

freed from the bondage of karma, and from its results
both pleasant and painful. Then, firm in renunciation
and yoga, with your heart free, you will come to me.

²⁹I look upon all creatures equally; none are less dear
to me and none more dear. But those who worship
me with love live in me, and I come to life in them.

³⁰Even sinners become holy when they take
refuge in me alone. ³¹Quickly their souls
conform to dharma and they attain to boundless
peace. Never forget this, Arjuna: no one who
is devoted to me will ever come to harm.

³²All those who take refuge in me, whatever their
birth, race, sex, or caste, will attain the supreme
goal; this realization can be attained even by those
whom society scorns. ³³Kings and sages too seek
this goal with devotion. Therefore, having been
born in this transient and forlorn world, give all
your love to me. ³⁴Fill your mind with me; love
me; serve me; worship me always. Seeking me in
your heart, you will at last be united with me.

⓾ *Divine Splendor*

KRISHNA GOES DEEPER into the revelation of his divine being, revealing himself as the source from which all things come, the One who is the reality behind the many. Though the source of all virtues, he is also the ultimate reality that transcends all opposites. Thus he is both happiness and suffering, birth and death, being and nonbeing. Like the Brahman of the Upanishads, he is beyond duality, utterly beyond the constricting categories of the things of this world. His true nature is beyond the reach of thought. He can only be known in the state of samadhi, where knower and known become one.

Arjuna calls Krishna *Purushottama,* "the supreme Purusha, the supreme Person." Krishna is now no human charioteer but Bhagavan, "the munificent Lord"; and Arjuna, leaving his warrior persona behind, now stands revealed as a seeker after truth. At Arjuna's request, Krishna now reveals a few of his divine powers and attributes (*vibhutis*).

From this point on the chapter becomes difficult because

of the many unfamiliar names that are mentioned. In whatever category, Krishna is the chief, the best, the most intense, the most beautiful, the most awesome, the essence. Many of the allusions will be familiar – for example, among rivers Krishna is the Ganges. But many of the names come from Hindu mythology and are not well known. There is no room here to explain every name, but the following paragraphs will highlight a few of importance.

First, Krishna is the Atman, the inner Self in all beings. It is fitting that this be mentioned first, for of all his myriad manifestations this is the most important, at least to the struggling spiritual aspirant that is Arjuna. Krishna is Arjuna's innermost Self, and that is how he is to be known in contemplation. Of all the forms in which to meditate upon Krishna, the Atman is mentioned first.

Krishna is Vishnu, the great compassionate, sustaining God of the Hindu faith. It is Vishnu who cares so much about the sufferings of Mother Earth and her children that he comes to earth again and again, in age after age, to relieve oppression and renew righteousness.

Krishna is the sun, worshipped in India since ancient times. He is Indra, the chief of the Vedic gods, the lord of storm and battle, who hurls the thunderbolt against the enemies of the gods. In Vedic religion he is a mighty lord, not to be trifled with, but later on he must admit defeat at the hands of Krishna, who protects the people from Indra's stormy wrath.

Krishna is also Shankara, the more beneficent aspect of the awesome deity Rudra, better known as Shiva. Among mountains Krishna is Meru, the high mountain home of Shiva and the other gods, the highest peak and center of the world. Krishna is consciousness, the syllable *Om,* and the mantram or holy name. He is the mythic horse and the fabulous elephant that were produced when the cosmic ocean was churned for the elixir of immortality.

Krishna is Ananta, the cosmic serpent on which Lord Vishnu sleeps. He is Varuna, Vedic god of the oceans, and Yama, the god of death; among demons (*asuras*) he is Prahlada, who, though born in the race of demons, was devoted to God and never swayed in his love, even when his own father tried to kill him. And of course Krishna is Rama, the great warrior-prince – also an incarnation of Vishnu – whose exploits are told in the immortal epic, the *Ramayana.*

Of all fields of knowledge, Krishna says, he is knowledge of the Self. The study of Sanskrit and its grammar were important in ancient India, and Krishna doesn't neglect this field. He is *A* among letters; among compound words he is the *dvandva,* which joins equals. He is the Gayatri – a particular meter found in the poetry of the Vedas, but generally taken to be a famous prayer from the Rig Veda (III.62.10) composed in that meter, which has been chanted every morning by count-less worshippers for three thousand years.

It is fitting that among seasons Krishna is the spring, the season of flowers. Less easily understood is his claim to be the gambling of gamblers. Krishna has a sense of play, and as gambling is the obsession of the gambler, it seems natural that Krishna might claim this as a *vibhuti*. Also, in ancient India gambling was considered a royal pastime, and no king of repute would refuse a friendly game of dice.

In the human realm, Krishna is the "son of Vasudeva," a prince of the Vrishni line – in other words, the human form that is Arjuna's friend and charioteer. He is also Arjuna! And he is Vyasa, the composer of the Gita – indeed, of the whole *Mahabharata*.

Wherever Arjuna finds strength, beauty, or power, Krishna concludes, he should recognize it as coming from a spark of Krishna's glory. Then, after overwhelming Arjuna with this stupendous list of divine powers and revelations, Krishna asks casually, "But what use is it to know all of these details? The important fact is to know that I am, and that a tiny portion of my being supports all things."

– D.M.

10 ◦ *Divine Splendor*

KRISHNA

¹Listen further, Arjuna, to my supreme teaching,
which gives you such joy. Desiring your welfare,
O strong-armed warrior, I will tell you more.

²Neither gods nor sages know my origin, for I
am the source from which the gods and sages
come. ³Whoever knows me as the Lord of all
creation, without birth or beginning, knows
the truth and frees himself from all evil.

⁴Discrimination, wisdom, understanding,
forgiveness, truth, self-control, and peace of
mind; pleasure and pain, birth and death, fear
and courage, honor and dishonor; ⁵nonviolence,
charity, equanimity, contentment, and perseverance
in spiritual disciplines – all the different qualities
found in living creatures have their source in me.

⁶The seven great sages and the four ancient
ancestors were born from my mind and received
my power. From them came all the creatures of
this world. ⁷Whoever understands my power
and the mystery of my manifestations comes
without doubt to be united with me.

⁸I am the source from which all creatures evolve.
The wise remember this and worship me with loving
devotion. ⁹Their thoughts are all absorbed in me, and
all their vitality flows to me. Teaching one another,
talking about me always, they are happy and fulfilled.

¹⁰To those steadfast in love and devotion I give
spiritual wisdom, so that they may come to me.
¹¹Out of compassion I destroy the darkness of their
ignorance. From within them I light the lamp of
wisdom and dispel all darkness from their lives.

ARJUNA

¹²You are Brahman supreme, the highest abode,
the supreme purifier, the self-luminous, eternal
spirit, first among the gods, unborn and infinite.
¹³The great sages and seers – Narada, Asita,
Devala, and Vyasa too – have acclaimed you
thus; now you have declared it to me yourself.

[14]Now, O Krishna, I believe that everything you
have told me is divine truth. O Lord, neither gods
nor demons know your real nature. [15]Indeed,
you alone know yourself, O supreme spirit. You
are the source of being and the master of every
creature, God of gods, the Lord of the universe.

[16]Tell me all your divine attributes, leaving
nothing unsaid. Tell me of the glories with which
you fill the cosmos. [17]Krishna, you are a supreme
master of yoga. Tell me how I should meditate
to gain constant awareness of you. In what things
and in what ways should I meditate on you?
[18]O Krishna, you who stir up people's hearts,
tell me in detail your attributes and your powers;
I can never tire of hearing your immortal words.

KRISHNA

[19]All right, Arjuna, I will tell you of my
divine powers. I will mention only the most
glorious; for there is no end to them.

[20]I am the true Self in the heart of every
creature, Arjuna, and the beginning,
middle, and end of their existence.

²¹Among the shining gods I am Vishnu; of
luminaries I am the sun; among the storm gods I
am Marichi, and in the night sky I am the moon.

²²Among scriptures I am the Sama Veda, and among
the lesser gods I am Indra. Among the senses I am
the mind, and in living beings I am consciousness.

²³Among the Rudras I am Shankara. Among
the spirits of the natural world I am Kubera,
god of wealth, and Pavaka, the purifying
fire. Among mountains I am Meru.

²⁴Among priests I am Brihaspati, and among
military leaders I am Skanda. Among
bodies of water I am the ocean.

²⁵Among the great seers I am Bhrigu, and among
words, the syllable *Om;* I am the repetition of the holy
name, and among mountains I am the Himalayas.

²⁶Among trees I am the *ashvattha,* the sacred fig;
among the *gandharvas,* the heavenly musicians,
I am Chitraratha. Among divine seers I am
Narada, and among sages I am Kapila.

27I was born from the nectar of immortality
as the primordial horse and as Indra's noble
elephant. Among human beings, I am the king.

28Among weapons I am the thunderbolt.
I am Kamadhuk, the cow that fulfills all
desires; I am Kandarpa, the power of sex,
and Vasuki, the king of snakes.

29I am Ananta, the cosmic serpent, and Varuna,
the god of water; I am Aryaman among the
noble ancestors. Among the forces which
restrain I am Yama, the god of death.

30Among animals I am the lion; among birds, the
eagle Garuda. I am Prahlada, born among the
demons, and of all that measures, I am time.

31Among purifying forces I am the wind; among
warriors, Rama. Of water creatures I am the
crocodile, and of rivers I am the Ganges.

32I am the beginning, middle, and end of creation.
Of all the sciences I am the science of Self-
knowledge, and I am logic in those who debate.
33Among letters I am A; among grammatical

compounds I am the *dvandva*. I am infinite time, and the sustainer whose face is seen everywhere.

[34]I am death, which overcomes all, and the source of all beings still to be born. I am the feminine qualities: fame, beauty, perfect speech, memory, intelligence, loyalty, and forgiveness.

[35]Among the hymns of the Sama Veda I am the Brihat; among poetic meters, the Gayatri. Among months I am Margashirsha, first of the year; among seasons I am spring, that brings forth flowers.

[36]I am the gambling of the gambler and the radiance in all that shines. I am effort, I am victory, and I am the goodness of the virtuous.

[37]Among the Vrishnis I am Krishna, and among the Pandavas I am Arjuna. Among sages I am Vyasa, and among poets, Ushanas.

[38]I am the scepter which metes out punishment, and the art of statesmanship in those who lead. I am the silence of the unknown and the wisdom of the wise.

[39]I am the seed that can be found in every creature, Arjuna; for without me nothing can exist, neither animate nor inanimate.

[40]But there is no end to my divine attributes, Arjuna; these I have mentioned are only a few. [41]Wherever you find strength, or beauty, or spiritual power, you may be sure that these have sprung from a spark of my essence.

[42]But of what use is it to you to know all this, Arjuna? Just remember that I am, and that I support the entire cosmos with only a fragment of my being.

▯: *The Cosmic Vision*

THIS IS THE most exalted chapter of the entire Gita, for here Arjuna sees the divine vision of Krishna in his full nature as God himself, Lord of the Universe. It is difficult to see at first why the ultimate spiritual vision should be granted to Arjuna at this point. We must remember that Krishna and Arjuna have been companions for many lives. Yet at the opening of the Gita, Arjuna is a warrior, little concerned with mystic visions. Step by step Krishna has led him to an understanding of the real purpose of his life – to know who he is and to know also who Krishna is. In the last chapter, Krishna had reached the point where he was willing to reveal to Arjuna the manifestations of divine power. Arjuna had not only asked about those powers, but had even wanted to know in which forms he might meditate on Krishna – the first time Arjuna had spoken of contemplation.

Now, in chapter 11, Arjuna asks to see Krishna as He really is. His desire is granted, and in essence the rest of the chapter describes Arjuna's samadhi. *Samadhi* is the word used by

Patanjali in his classic work, the *Yoga Sutras,* to describe the final stage in meditation, in which the mind is completely concentrated and a superconscious mode of knowing comes into play. Patanjali speaks of many different kinds of samadhi, but for practical purposes we may speak of two: *savikalpa* and *nirvikalpa.* Arjuna's vision begins with savikalpa samadhi, in which he sees God in a personal manifestation. Then, as he passes into nirvikalpa samadhi, Arjuna sees all forms disappearing into God, until only a supernatural fire consuming the entire phenomenal world is left.

This supreme vision dazzles Arjuna with the blinding splendor of a thousand suns. Mystics have often described their experiences in terms of light. In an ancient prayer of the Veda, the poet asks for divine wisdom to dawn in his heart just as the sun rises in the sky. And in the West we have countless testimonies like that of St. Teresa of Avila:

> When the soul looks upon this Divine Sun, the brightness dazzles it. . . . And very often it remains completely blind, absorbed, amazed, and dazzled by all the wonders it sees.

As this vision begins to unfold, Arjuna sees the whole world in the body of Krishna and he begins a hymn of praise. He sees Krishna as Vishnu with his traditional weapons, the mace and the discus, and wearing a crown.

As the vision becomes more intense, Arjuna begins to feel afraid. He sees the light of God become a fire that burns to consume all things, as if at the end of time. All the warriors on the battlefield are mortals, and Arjuna sees them slain, burning in the universal fire. All creatures rush to destruction like moths into a flame. God's radiance is both a great light and a burning fire.

Terrified, Arjuna wants to know the identity of this awesome God, who bears no resemblance now to the Krishna he had known as his teacher and friend. In answer to the question, "Who are you?" Krishna's reply is the verse (11:32) that burst into Robert Oppenheimer's mind when he saw the atomic bomb explode over Trinity in the summer of 1945: "I am become Death, the shatterer of worlds. . . ." But the word *kala* means not just death but time, which eventually devours all.

Arjuna is brave, and worthy of this vision, for he does not lose consciousness or completely break down. He praises Krishna and then asks for forgiveness if during their long friendship he has ever said or done anything to offend the Lord through mistaking him for a mere human being. Finally, the vision is too much for Arjuna. Though he experiences the deep peace and joy of samadhi, he is terrified at the same time. He wishes to see the more human face of God.

Krishna grants his desire and returns to his gentle, normal aspect. He tells Arjuna how very difficult it is to see him in his exalted form as the Lord of Yoga, the God of gods. Only pure devotion attains this vision. This theme dominates the remaining chapters of the Gita: it is devotion that is all-important on the spiritual quest.

– D.M.

11 ◊ *The Cosmic Vision*

ARJUNA

¹Out of compassion you have taught me the
supreme mystery of the Self. Through your words
my delusion is gone. ²You have explained the origin
and end of every creature, O lotus-eyed one, and
told me of your own supreme, limitless existence.

³Just as you have described your infinite glory,
O Lord, now I long to see it. I want to see you
as the supreme ruler of creation. ⁴O Lord,
master of yoga, if you think me strong enough
to behold it, show me your immortal Self.

KRISHNA

⁵Behold, Arjuna, a million divine forms, with an
infinite variety of color and shape. ⁶Behold the gods
of the natural world, and many more wonders never
revealed before. ⁷Behold the entire cosmos turning
within my body, and the other things you desire to see.

⁸But these things cannot be seen with your
physical eyes; therefore I give you spiritual
vision to perceive my majestic power.

SANJAYA

⁹Having spoken these words, Krishna, the master of
yoga, revealed to Arjuna his most exalted, lordly form.

¹⁰He appeared with an infinite number of faces,
ornamented by heavenly jewels, displaying unending
miracles and the countless weapons of his power.
¹¹Clothed in celestial garments and covered with
garlands, sweet-smelling with heavenly fragrances,
he showed himself as the infinite Lord, the source
of all wonders, whose face is everywhere.

¹²If a thousand suns were to rise in the heavens
at the same time, the blaze of their light would
resemble the splendor of that supreme spirit.

¹³There, within the body of the God of gods,
Arjuna saw all the manifold forms of the universe
united as one. ¹⁴Filled with amazement, his hair
standing on end in ecstasy, he bowed before the
Lord with joined palms and spoke these words.

ARJUNA

¹⁵O Lord, I see within your body all the
gods and every kind of living creature. I see
Brahma, the Creator, seated on a lotus; I see
the ancient sages and the celestial serpents.

¹⁶I see infinite mouths and arms, stomachs
and eyes, and you are embodied in every form.
I see you everywhere, without beginning,
middle, or end. You are the Lord of all
creation, and the cosmos is your body.

¹⁷You wear a crown and carry a mace and discus;
your radiance is blinding and immeasurable. I
see you, who are so difficult to behold, shining
like a fiery sun blazing in every direction.

¹⁸You are the supreme, changeless Reality,
the one thing to be known. You are the
refuge of all creation, the immortal spirit,
the eternal guardian of eternal dharma.

¹⁹You are without beginning, middle, or end;
you touch everything with your infinite power.

The sun and moon are your eyes, and your mouth
is fire; your radiance warms the cosmos.

²⁰O Lord, your presence fills the heavens and
the earth and reaches in every direction. I see
the three worlds trembling before this vision
of your wonderful and terrible form.

²¹The gods enter your being, some calling
out and greeting you in fear. Great saints sing
your glory, praying, "May all be well!"

²²The multitudes of gods, demigods, and demons
are all overwhelmed by the sight of you. ²³O
mighty Lord, at the sight of your myriad eyes
and mouths, arms and legs, stomachs and fearful
teeth, I and the entire universe shake in terror.

²⁴O Vishnu, I can see your eyes shining; with open
mouth, you glitter in an array of colors, and your
body touches the sky. I look at you and my heart
trembles; I have lost all courage and all peace of mind.

²⁵When I see your mouths with their fearful teeth,
mouths burning like the fires at the end of time,

I forget where I am and I have no place to go. O Lord,
you are the support of the universe; have mercy on me!

26I see all the sons of Dhritarashtra; I see Bhishma,
Drona, and Karna; I see our warriors and all the kings
who are here to fight. **27**All are rushing into your awful
jaws; I see some of them crushed by your teeth. **28**As
rivers flow into the ocean, all the warriors of this
world are passing into your fiery jaws; **29**all creatures
rush to their destruction like moths into a flame.

30You lap the worlds into your burning mouths and
swallow them. Filled with your terrible radiance,
O Vishnu, the whole of creation bursts into flames.

31Tell me who you are, O Lord of terrible form.
I bow before you; have mercy! I want to know
who you are, you who existed before all creation.
Your nature and workings confound me.

KRISHNA

32I am time, the destroyer of all; I have come to
consume the world. Even without your participation,
all the warriors gathered here will die.

³³Therefore arise, Arjuna; conquer your enemies and
enjoy the glory of sovereignty. I have already slain
all these warriors; you will only be my instrument.

³⁴Bhishma, Drona, Jayadratha, Karna, and
many others are already slain. Kill those whom
I have killed. Do not hesitate. Fight in this
battle and you will conquer your enemies.

SANJAYA

³⁵Having heard these words, Arjuna trembled
in fear. With joined palms he bowed before
Krishna and addressed him stammering.

ARJUNA

³⁶O Krishna, it is right that the world delights
and rejoices in your praise, that all the saints
and sages bow down to you and all evil flees
before you to the far corners of the universe.

³⁷How could they not worship you, O Lord? You
are the eternal spirit, who existed before Brahma
the Creator and who will never cease to be. Lord
of the gods, you are the abode of the universe.
Changeless, you are what is and what is not, and
beyond the duality of existence and nonexistence.

³⁸You are the first among the gods, the timeless spirit, the resting place of all beings. You are the knower and the thing which is known. You are the final home; with your infinite form you pervade the cosmos.

³⁹You are Vayu, god of wind; Yama, god of death; Agni, god of fire; Varuna, god of water. You are the moon and the creator Prajapati, and the great-grandfather of all creatures. I bow before you and salute you again and again.

⁴⁰You are behind me and in front of me; I bow to you on every side. Your power is immeasurable. You pervade everything; you are everything.

⁴¹Sometimes, because we were friends, I rashly said, "Oh, Krishna! Say, friend!" – casual, careless remarks. Whatever I may have said lightly, whether we were playing or resting, alone or in company, sitting together or eating, ⁴²if it was disrespectful, forgive me for it, O Krishna. I did not know the greatness of your nature, unchanging and imperishable.

⁴³You are the father of the universe, of the animate and the inanimate; you are the object of

all worship, the greatest guru. There is none to equal you in the three worlds. Who can match your power? **⁴⁴**O gracious Lord, I prostrate myself before you and ask for your blessing. As a father forgives his son, or a friend a friend, or a lover his beloved, so should you forgive me.

⁴⁵I rejoice in seeing you as you have never been seen before, yet I am filled with fear by this vision of you as the abode of the universe. Please let me see you again as the shining God of gods. **⁴⁶**Though you are the embodiment of all creation, let me see you again not with a thousand arms but with four, carrying the mace and discus and wearing a crown.

KRISHNA

⁴⁷Arjuna, through my grace you have been united with me and received this vision of my radiant, universal form, without beginning or end, which no one else has ever seen.

⁴⁸Not by knowledge of the Vedas, nor sacrifice, nor charity, nor rituals, nor even by severe asceticism has any other mortal seen what you have seen, O heroic Arjuna.

⁴⁹Do not be troubled; do not fear my terrible
form. Let your heart be satisfied and your fears
dispelled in looking at me as I was before.

SANJAYA

⁵⁰Having spoken these words, the Lord once
again assumed the gentle form of Krishna and
consoled his devotee, who had been so afraid.

ARJUNA

⁵¹O Krishna, now that I have seen your
gentle human form my mind is again
composed and returned to normal.

KRISHNA

⁵²It is extremely difficult to obtain the vision you
have had; even the gods long always to see me in
this aspect. ⁵³Neither knowledge of the Vedas, nor
austerity, nor charity, nor sacrifice can bring the vision
you have seen. ⁵⁴But through unfailing devotion,
Arjuna, you can know me, see me, and attain union
with me. ⁵⁵Those who make me the supreme goal
of all their work and act without selfish attachment,
who devote themselves to me completely and are
free from ill will for any creature, enter into me.

ⅠⅠ: *The Way of Love*

THIS SHORT CHAPTER focuses upon the supreme importance of devotion and faith in spiritual development. Here love, or personal devotion, is the most powerful motivation in spiritual life.

The world's great religions agree on this point. All religions allow for a way of devotion, and millions of men and women have found spiritual fulfillment in devotion to Christ, the Buddha, or Muhammad. Hinduism has allowed a place for the path of knowledge as well as the path of devotion; here, however, the Gita stresses the efficacy of devotion.

The Upanishads, the final word on mystic experience uttered by the Vedas, stressed the ultimate reality, the eternal truth behind the ephemeral things of this world. The teachers of the Upanishads told their students to seek knowledge of the Atman, their true Self. The consummation of this knowledge was to know that the Self within was one with Brahman, the ultimate reality pervading all things. This was encapsulated in the statement *Tat tvam asi,* "You are that" – that imperishable being, that immortal Reality. Brahman, the nameless, formless Godhead, could be known only in the superconscious state.

The Gita moves away from such an approach to religion. For as Krishna says, seeking an eternal, indefinable, hidden Godhead is rather a tall order for the average (or even above average) person. In fact, in this chapter it is said to be beyond the reach of practically all "embodied beings" (*deha-vat,* "those who have bodies"). This path of wisdom may be just too "spiritual" for earth's children, because those who identify to a large degree with their physical nature find the way of knowledge too steep a climb. We can turn to one of the Western followers of this path to see why; this is Dionysius the Areopagite, a Christian monk of the fifth century, sounding remarkably like verses 3–4 of this very chapter:

> Then, beyond all distinction between knower and known,
> the aspirant becomes merged in the nameless, formless
> Reality, wholly absorbed in That which is beyond all things
> and in nothing else. . . . Having stilled his intellect and
> mind, he is united by his highest faculty with That which is
> beyond all knowing.

Fortunately there is the path of love; for when God is loved in personal aspect, the way is vastly easier. According to the Hindu scriptures, God can be loved as a merciful father, a divine mother, a wise friend, a passionate beloved, or even as a mischievous child.

We might turn to the Christian mystics for help here, for most of them have walked the way of love. The medieval Christian work called *The Cloud of Unknowing* states that love is the sure, safe path to God: "By love He can be gotten and holden, by thought never." In a well-known passage in the New Testament, St. Paul puts love above knowledge and even above miraculous powers: "But I shall give you a more excellent way. . . . Love never faileth. But whether there be prophecies, they shall fail. Whether there be tongues, they shall cease. Whether there be knowledge, it shall vanish away." And St. John of the Cross tells concisely why the vast majority of human beings find it easier to overcome their weaknesses through love than through knowledge:

> In order to overcome our desires and to renounce all those things, our love and inclination for which are wont to inflame the will that it delights therein, we require a more ardent fire and a nobler love – that of the Bridegroom. . . . if our spiritual nature were not on fire with other and nobler passions, we should never cast off the yoke of the senses.

But such love is often not forthcoming in the struggling soul, even in one like Arjuna. So Krishna says that if Arjuna is not able to focus his devotion, he should learn to do so through the regular practice of meditation. Even love and devotion can be cultivated through regular practice; they needn't be regarded as mysterious forces, divine gifts of the spirit.

If even the attempt at regular practice should fail, Krishna is still not ready to let Arjuna admit defeat. He should, Krishna says, work selflessly without desire for the fruits of his labors. But real peace of mind comes only from renunciation. The word *tyaga* here seems to mean renunciation or abandonment of self-will more than anything else. Such self-surrender may be a last resort, but if it is genuine it brings immediate peace.

Verses 13–20 describe the characteristics of the genuine lover of God. Such a saintly person, Krishna points out, is greatly loved and dear to Krishna himself.

– D.M.

12 ☷ *The Way of Love*

ARJUNA

[1]Of those steadfast devotees who love you and
those who seek you as the eternal formless
Reality, who are the more established in yoga?

KRISHNA

[2]Those who set their hearts on me and
worship me with unfailing devotion and
faith are more established in yoga.

[3]As for those who seek the transcendental Reality,
without name, without form, contemplating
the Unmanifested, beyond the reach of thought
and of feeling, [4]with their senses subdued and
mind serene and striving for the good of all
beings, they too will verily come unto me.

[5]Yet hazardous and slow is the path to the Unrevealed,
difficult for physical creatures to tread. [6]But they

for whom I am the supreme goal, who do all work
renouncing self for me and meditate on me with
single-hearted devotion, ⁷these I will swiftly rescue
from the fragment's cycle of birth and death,
for their consciousness has entered into me.

⁸Still your mind in me, still your intellect in me, and
without doubt you will be united with me forever.
⁹If you cannot still your mind in me, learn to do so
through the regular practice of meditation. ¹⁰If you
lack the will for such self-discipline, engage yourself
in my work, for selfless service can lead you at last to
complete fulfillment. ¹¹If you are unable to do even
this, surrender yourself to me, disciplining yourself
and renouncing the results of all your actions.

¹²Better indeed is knowledge than mechanical
practice. Better than knowledge is meditation.
But better still is surrender of attachment to
results, because there follows immediate peace.

¹³That one I love who is incapable of ill will, who
is friendly and compassionate. Living beyond
the reach of "I" and "mine" and of pleasure and
pain, ¹⁴patient, contented, self-controlled, firm

in faith, with all their heart and all their mind
given to me – with such as these I am in love.

15Not agitating the world or by it agitated, they
stand above the sway of elation, competition,
and fear: that one is my beloved.

16They are detached, pure, efficient, impartial,
never anxious, selfless in all their undertakings;
they are my devotees, very dear to me.

17That one is dear to me who runs not after the
pleasant or away from the painful, grieves not, lusts
not, but lets things come and go as they happen.

18That devotee who looks upon friend and foe with
equal regard, who is not buoyed up by praise nor
cast down by blame, alike in heat and cold, pleasure
and pain, free from selfish attachments, 19the same
in honor and dishonor, quiet, ever full, in harmony
everywhere, firm in faith – such a one is dear to me.

20Those who meditate upon this immortal
dharma as I have declared it, full of faith and
seeking me as life's supreme goal, are truly my
devotees, and my love for them is very great.

⬛ *The Field & the Knower*

THIS CHAPTER PRESENTS us with two sweeping categories: the "field" and the "knower of the field." To simplify, we may think of the field as the body and the knower of the field as the Self that resides in the body. This chapter, then, is about the duality between "soul and body." This duality is seen as eternal, a basic division of all things – a fundamental concept elaborated in Sankhya philosophy.

We said that the "field" is the body, but this is not precise enough. The field also includes the mind: in fact, it comprises all the components of prakriti including *ahamkara* – the awareness each of us has that we are an individual ego, from *aham* "I" and *kara* "maker." Ahamkara is the basic awareness of separateness: that which makes me "I," a being separate from the rest of creation. In this wide sense the field encompasses everything, except for the elusive consciousness that "knows" the field. The field is the object; the knower is the subject. Krishna is the hidden knower of the field: that is, the Self.

This term "field" is a surprisingly modern one, for it describes what today we might call an extension of the continuum of mass, energy, time, and space to include the strata of mind as well – in other words, a field of forces both physical and mental. Just as physics no longer regards matter and energy as essentially separate, the Gita would not regard matter and mind as separate; they are different aspects of prakriti, the underlying "stuff" of existence.

Another dimension of Krishna's use of the word "field" is brought out by a traditional Hindu anecdote. A wandering *sadhu* or holy man is asked what his work in life is; he replies, "I'm a farmer." When the questioner looks surprised he adds, "This body of mine is my field. I sow good thoughts and actions, and in my body I reap the results." The Buddha explains, "All that we are is the result of what we have thought: it is founded on our thoughts; it is made of our thoughts." What we think, we become, for as Emerson says, the ancestor of every action is a thought. Thus our thoughts, taken together, bear fruit in the actions, decisions, and desires that shape our lives. In part, the body bears the fruit of what we think insofar as our way of thinking affects our health and safety. But in a larger sense, the whole field of human activity (indeed the whole of prakriti) is also a "field of karma" – where, for example, the global environment is shaped by the sum of what its inhabitants do, which in turn is shaped by how they think. This idea will be picked up and elaborated on in detail in the concluding chapters of the Gita.

Verses 7–11 then describe the person who understands his or her own true nature. This is an attractive picture of the modest, truly wise person who is in control of his or her own life. One implication of these verses is that it is quite an achievement to understand the difference between the field and the Self, the knower. Most people confuse the two, taking the body and mind to be who they are. In the usual course of events, we may be totally unaware that there is a Self, a consciousness underneath the surface awareness of a separate "I." Verses 12–17 describe the ultimate underlying reality: Brahman, pure, undifferentiated consciousness, the divine ground of existence.

Verse 19 returns us to the discussion of the basic duality of mind/matter and spirit (Self). Again the technical terms *prakriti* and *Purusha* are used. Purusha is the knower and prakriti the field. From the union of these two all things are born. Both prakriti and Purusha are essential to the creation of the world: nothing could exist without the spiritual basis of Purusha, and nothing could develop in a manifest form without the mind and matter of prakriti.

With its need to think of abstract principles in human terms, Hinduism embodies these two eternal principles in the figures of Shiva and Shakti, the divine Father and Mother. The

Gita does not mention these two because it comes essentially from the Vishnu tradition, but in the other great stream of the Hindu faith, Shiva is the eternal Spirit, the Absolute, represented as dwelling aloof on the mountain peak of spiritual peace. Shakti, the Divine Mother, is his creative partner, and without her, Shiva could never have created the world. Shakti – she has many names in her various manifestations – rules in the realm of birth and death; Shiva, Purusha, lives in the realm of the immortal. Together the two represent Brahman, the attributeless Godhead, and the creative power of the Godhead called maya. Thus it is in the union of Shiva and Shakti that all things are born.

This chapter emphasizes that the Self, the real knower, is ever uninvolved in the shifting forces that play over the field. There is no possibility of any soul being eternally lost, for all beings partake of the immortal, pure nature of Purusha. We may endure countless eons of birth and death, but we must finally find our rest in the eternal spirit. By definition, nothing taking place in the realm of prakriti can affect Purusha; but the exact nature of the interaction of these two is a profound mystery.

Verse 32 explains this mystery by drawing a comparison with *akasha,* the subtlest element recognized by the ancient philosophers. Akasha is space itself. Just as space pervades the cosmos, yet remains pure even in the midst of impure things, so the Self remains completely pure, even though it dwells in all things. Though it seems to live in the land of mortals and to undergo change and death, the real knower in every creature is deathless, "hidden in the heart."

– D.M.

13 ❧ *The Field & the Knower*

KRISHNA

¹The body is called a field, Arjuna; the one who
knows it is called the Knower of the field. This
is the knowledge of those who know. ²I am the
Knower of the field in everyone, Arjuna. Knowledge
of the field and its Knower is true knowledge.

³Listen and I will explain the nature of the field
and how change takes place within it. I will
also describe the Knower of the field and his
power. ⁴These truths have been sung by great
sages in a variety of ways, and expounded in
precise arguments concerning Brahman.

⁵The field, Arjuna, is made up of the following: the five
areas of sense perception; the five elements; the five
sense organs and the five organs of action; the three
components of the mind: *manas, buddhi,* and
ahamkara; and the undifferentiated energy from

which all these evolved. ⁶In this field arise desire and aversion, pleasure and pain, the body, intelligence, and will.

⁷Those who know truly are free from pride and deceit. They are gentle, forgiving, upright, and pure, devoted to their spiritual teacher, filled with inner strength, and self-controlled. ⁸Detached from sense objects and self-will, they have learned the painful lesson of separate birth and suffering, old age, disease, and death.

⁹Free from selfish attachment, they do not get compulsively entangled even in home and family. They are even-minded through good fortune and bad. ¹⁰Their devotion to me is undivided. Enjoying solitude and not following the crowd, they seek only me. ¹¹This is true knowledge, to seek the Self as the true end of wisdom always. To seek anything else is ignorance.

¹²I will tell you of the wisdom that leads to immortality: the beginningless Brahman, which can be called neither being nor non-being.

¹³It dwells in all, in every hand and foot and head, in every mouth and eye and ear in the universe. ¹⁴Without senses itself, it shines through the

functioning of the senses. Completely independent, it supports all things. Beyond the gunas, it enjoys their play.

¹⁵ It is both near and far, both within and without every creature; it moves and is unmoving. ¹⁶ In its subtlety it is beyond comprehension. It is indivisible, yet appears divided in separate creatures. Know it to be the creator, the preserver, and the destroyer.

¹⁷ Dwelling in every heart, it is beyond darkness. It is called the light of light, the object and goal of knowledge, and knowledge itself.

¹⁸ I have revealed to you the nature of the field and the meaning and object of true knowledge. Those who are devoted to me, knowing these things, are united with me.

¹⁹ Know that prakriti and Purusha are both without beginning, and that from prakriti come the gunas and all that changes. ²⁰ Prakriti is the agent, cause, and effect of every action, but it is Purusha that seems to experience pleasure and pain.

21 Purusha, resting in prakriti, witnesses the play of
the gunas born of prakriti. But attachment to the
gunas leads a person to be born for good or evil.

22 Within the body the supreme Purusha
is called the witness, approver, supporter,
enjoyer, the supreme Lord, the highest Self.

23 Whoever realizes the true nature of Purusha,
prakriti, and the gunas, whatever path he or
she may follow, is not born separate again.

24 Some realize the Self within them through the
practice of meditation, some by the path of wisdom,
and others by selfless service. 25 Others may not know
these paths; but hearing and following the instructions
of an illumined teacher, they too go beyond death.

26 Whatever exists, Arjuna, animate or inanimate, is
born through the union of the field and its Knower.

27 They alone see truly who see the Lord the
same in every creature, who see the deathless
in the hearts of all that die. 28 Seeing the same
Lord everywhere, they do not harm themselves
or others. Thus they attain the supreme goal.

²⁹They alone see truly who see that all actions
are performed by prakriti, while the Self remains
unmoved. ³⁰When they see the variety of
creation rooted in that unity and growing out
of it, they attain fulfillment in Brahman.

³¹This supreme Self is without a beginning,
undifferentiated, deathless. Though it dwells in
the body, Arjuna, it neither acts nor is touched
by action. ³²As akasha pervades the cosmos
but remains unstained, the Self can never be
tainted though it dwells in every creature.

³³As the sun lights up the world, the Self dwelling in
the field is the source of all light in the field. ³⁴Those
who, with the eye of wisdom, distinguish the field
from its Knower and the way to freedom from the
bondage of prakriti, attain the supreme goal.

☱ *The Forces of Evolution*

THE LAST CHAPTER gave us the distinction between Purusha and prakriti. This chapter will tell us in more detail about the nature of prakriti – the basis of the world of mind and matter. Here the Gita explains human experience in terms of the three qualities of prakriti, known as *gunas: sattva, rajas,* and *tamas.* When the soul attains illumination it goes beyond the confines of prakriti into the spiritual realm of Purusha. But until then, the soul must learn to deal with these three all-powerful forces.

No single English word can be given to translate the words *sattva, rajas,* and *tamas.* The quality of sattva combines goodness, purity, light, harmony, balance. In terms of evolution, sattva is on the highest level. Rajas is energy – or, on the human level, passion – which can be both good and bad. In personality rajas may express itself in anger, hatred, or greed; but it also provides motivation, the will to act. Rajas is ambitious, which is not altogether a bad thing for the evolution of the soul. It is definitely superior to the third guna, tamas, which combines inertia, sloth, darkness, ignorance, insensitivity. This is the lowest state in terms of evolution; for tamas means a dead stability, where nothing much happens for good or ill. Worse, tamas can mean not just stability but a sliding backwards in the struggle of evolution, where to stand still may mean to be left behind (14:18).

In any given personality or phenomenon all the three gunas are likely to be present. It is the mix of the three that colors our experience. Sattva may be dominant, with an admixture of rajas or tamas. Or perhaps rajas dominates, with a little sattva and a good measure of tamas. Finally, the personality may be basically tamasic, with a few rays of the light of sattva and a little of the heat of rajas. In any case, no mix of the three gunas is stable, for it is the very nature of prakriti to be in constant flux. The gunas are constantly shifting, always changing in intensity.

It is essential that the gunas, even the purity and goodness of sattva, be transcended if the soul is to attain its final release. For the three gunas are forces that operate within the world of prakriti: in fact, their three strands make up the whole fabric of the phenomenal world. Liberation lies beyond the conditioning of prakriti, in the realm of Purusha. When Arjuna asks Krishna to describe the person who has gone beyond prakriti's net, Krishna replies that such a person is detached from the constant shifting and interaction of the gunas. Identified with the Self, he or she realizes that the gunas and their play are external – even the emotions and thoughts that seem so personal, so interior, are really only the play of prakriti. Thoughts and emotions, and ahamkara itself, stop at the gate of the inner Self. The Self abides in the inner chamber of the heart, always at peace, whatever forces of prakriti may storm outside. The illumined man or woman maintains a joyful evenness of mind in happiness and sorrow.

At the end of the chapter, again reminding him of the power of devotion (*bhakti*), Krishna says that Arjuna can transcend the gunas through steadfast love. If he has devotion and has gone beyond the three gunas, then he will be fit to know Brahman.

– D.M.

14 II: *The Forces of Evolution*

[1]Let me tell you more about the wisdom that transcends all knowledge, through which the saints and sages attained perfection. [2]Those who rely on this wisdom will be united with me. For them there is neither rebirth nor fear of death.

[3]My womb is prakriti; in that I place the seed. Thus all created things are born. [4]Everything born, Arjuna, comes from the womb of prakriti, and I am the seed-giving father.

[5]It is the three gunas born of prakriti – sattva, rajas, and tamas – that bind the immortal Self to the body. [6]Sattva – pure, luminous, and free from sorrow – binds us with attachment to happiness and wisdom. [7]Rajas is passion, arising from selfish desire and attachment. These bind the Self with compulsive

action. [8]Tamas, born of ignorance, deludes all
creatures through heedlessness, indolence, and sleep.

[9]Sattva binds us to happiness; rajas
binds us to action. Tamas, distorting our
understanding, binds us to delusion.

[10]Sattva predominates when rajas and tamas
are transformed. Rajas prevails when sattva
is weak and tamas overcome. Tamas prevails
when rajas and sattva are dormant.

[11]When sattva predominates, the light of wisdom
shines through every gate of the body. [12]When
rajas predominates, a person runs about pursuing
selfish and greedy ends, driven by restlessness and
desire. [13]When tamas is dominant a person lives in
darkness – slothful, confused, and easily infatuated.

[14]Those dying in the state of sattva attain the pure
worlds of the wise. [15]Those dying in rajas are reborn
among people driven by work. But those who die in
tamas are conceived in the wombs of the ignorant.

¹⁶ The fruit of good deeds is pure and sattvic. The fruit of rajas is suffering. The fruit of tamas is ignorance and insensitivity.

¹⁷ From sattva comes understanding; from rajas, greed. But the outcome of tamas is confusion, infatuation, and ignorance.

¹⁸ Those who live in sattva go upwards; those in rajas remain where they are. But those immersed in tamas sink downwards.

¹⁹ The wise see clearly that all action is the work of the gunas. Knowing that which is above the gunas, they enter into union with me.

²⁰ Going beyond the three gunas which form the body, they leave behind the cycle of birth and death, decrepitude and sorrow, and attain to immortality.

ARJUNA

²¹ What are the characteristics of those who have gone beyond the gunas, O Lord? How do they act? How have they passed beyond the gunas' hold?

KRISHNA

²² They are unmoved by the harmony of sattva, the activity of rajas, or the delusion of tamas. They feel no aversion when these forces are active, nor do they crave for them when these forces subside.

²³ They remain impartial, undisturbed by the actions of the gunas. Knowing that it is the gunas which act, they abide within themselves and do not vacillate.

²⁴ Established within themselves, they are equal in pleasure and pain, praise and blame, kindness and unkindness. Clay, a rock, and gold are the same to them. ²⁵ Alike in honor and dishonor, alike to friend and foe, they have given up every selfish pursuit. Such are those who have gone beyond the gunas.

²⁶ By serving me with steadfast love, a man or woman goes beyond the gunas. Such a one is fit for union with Brahman. ²⁷ For I am the support of Brahman, the eternal, the unchanging, the deathless, the everlasting dharma, the source of all joy.

▣ The Supreme Self

THIS IS A difficult chapter, for it deals essentially with questions of theology and ultimate mystical experience.

Krishna reveals that he transcends not only the world of matter but also the immortal Atman that dwells as the conscious "knower" within all beings. Krishna has said that he is the Atman; but the paradox is that he also transcends the Atman. In this highest aspect Krishna is Ishvara, the cosmic Lord, who abides in his own mystery. The liberated Self enjoys union with Krishna and lives in Krishna's highest home. But the Self does not become Krishna: the immortal soul, even when liberated from its mortal journeying, does not become God.

The chapter opens with the image of an upside-down tree, a world-tree rooted in Brahman which branches out into a manifold creation in this realm below. This is said to be an *ashvattha* or pipal tree, a kind of fig. Like the banyan, it sends out roots into the air, spreading above and below.

In this chapter about Krishna's most exalted nature, it

is appropriate that his "home," the highest goal of all, is described. It is an abode of light and eternal life. By its very nature, it is beyond the description of human language. Verse 4 uses an elemental and ancient word for the ultimate reality that defies all description, all human thought: *Tat*, which means simply "that" or "it." Here the Gita personalizes Tat to the extent of giving It a home: *avyayam padam,* the immortal home, the eternal goal. *Pada* also means foot or step, and it is of interest here to recall a myth from the Vedas. At the beginning of time Vishnu took three steps that measured out the entire cosmos. The third and highest step became a heavenly world, the realm of the blessed. In the Rig Veda (1.154.5), the poet longs to find himself in this home of the god:

> May I go to his blessed world
> Where those who love the gods rejoice;
> For there, truly, is the company of the far-stepping god,
> A fountain of honey in the highest step of Vishnu.

The Gita describes Krishna's home as a realm of light beyond the light of the sun (15:6). Here we might compare the Gita with the Katha Upanishad (5:15):

> There shines not the sun, neither moon nor star,
> Nor flash of lightning, nor fire lit on earth.
> The Self is the light reflected by all.
> He shining, everything shines after him.

Even here, though, we are reminded that Krishna lives not just in this highest realm but also in the world below, where both darkness and light coexist. In his divine mystery he sends fragments of himself to become the inner Self in each creature. In this sense the Self enters the body at conception, dwells in the body, and then departs at death. Krishna is the prana – the breath or vitality – of the body. The Upanishads speak of five pranas; here the Gita mentions the two most prominent: the prana by which we breathe and the prana that digests food.

– D.M.

15 ॥ *The Supreme Self*

KRISHNA

[1]Sages speak of the immutable ashvattha
tree, with its taproot above and its branches
below. On this tree grow the scriptures; seeing
their source, one knows their essence.

[2]Nourished by the gunas, the limbs of this
tree spread above and below. Sense objects
grow on the limbs as buds; the roots hanging
down bind us to action in this world.

[3]The true form of this tree – its essence, beginning,
and end – is not perceived on this earth. Cut
down this strong-rooted tree with the sharp ax
of detachment; [4]then find the path which does
not come back again. Seek That, the First Cause,
from which the universe came long ago.

[5]Not deluded by pride, free from selfish attachment

and selfish desire, beyond the duality of pleasure
and pain, ever aware of the Self, the wise go
forward to that eternal goal. ⁶Neither the sun
nor the moon nor fire can add to that light.
This is my supreme abode, and those who enter
there do not return to separate existence.

⁷An eternal part of me enters into the world,
assuming the powers of action and perception
and a mind made of prakriti. ⁸When the divine
Self enters and leaves a body, it takes these along
as the wind carries a scent from place to place.
⁹Using the mind, ears, eyes, nose, and the senses
of taste and touch, the Self enjoys sense objects.

¹⁰The deluded do not see the Self when it leaves the
body or when it dwells within it. They do not see
the Self enjoying sense objects or acting through the
gunas. But they who have the eye of wisdom see.

¹¹Those who strive resolutely on the path of
yoga see the Self within. The thoughtless,
who strive imperfectly, do not.

¹²The brightness of the sun, which lights up the world,
the brightness of the moon and of fire – these are my

glory. [13] With a drop of my energy I enter the earth and
support all creatures. Through the moon, the vessel of
life-giving fluid, I nourish all plants. [14] I enter breathing
creatures and dwell within as the life-giving breath.
I am the fire in the stomach which digests all food.

[15] Entering into every heart, I give the power
to remember and understand; it is I again who
take that power away. All the scriptures lead
to me; I am their author and their wisdom.

[16] In this world there are two orders of being: the
perishable, separate creature and the changeless
spirit. [17] But beyond these there is another, the
supreme Self, the eternal Lord, who enters into
the entire cosmos and supports it from within.

[18] I am that supreme Self, praised by the scriptures
as beyond the changing and the changeless. [19] Those
who see in me that supreme Self see truly. They
have found the source of all wisdom, Arjuna,
and they worship me with all their heart.

[20] I have shared this profound truth with you,
Arjuna. Those who understand it will attain wisdom;
they will have done that which has to be done.

◻ *Two Paths*

IN THIS MOST unusual chapter, the Gita departs from a lofty view of human nature and describes two opposing forces. The higher tendency, the divine, leads to increasing happiness in the course of the soul's evolution, and eventually to its liberation; but there is also a downward current leading to suffering and enslavement of the spirit. This chapter is unusual in giving equal, if not in fact more, attention to this dark side of human nature. Here we get a detailed description of the divine qualities that liberate and the "demonic" qualities that enslave (16:5).

In a rare somber tone, Krishna describes the sinful person, the individual of a demonic kind – and it seems he knows what he is talking about. But first he assures Arjuna that he is of the divine type, so he shouldn't be alarmed.

The "demonic" personality is basically atheistic. For such people life does not originate in God or a divine reality but is grounded in biology, in sexual desire. Taking a low view of human nature, such people cause suffering to themselves as well as others. They are arrogant and have many insatiable selfish desires, and they do not hesitate to do anything that will get them what they want. Krishna grants that they may attain their desires, enjoying wealth and power, but their destination is hell – a hell of their own making, often in this very life, as their karma bears fruit.

One of the least likable characteristics of "demonic" personalities is their sense of self-importance. They like to give gifts ostentatiously and offer ritual sacrifices; this legitimizes their wealth and makes them feel respectable and esteemed. They like being generous if it will make them look good.

Krishna does not disguise his aversion to cruel people. He tells Arjuna that he arranges for them to be born again and again in a harsh world. Such souls cannot seem to purify their sinful hearts; repeating the same selfish ways, they sink lower and lower. This is a bleak picture, which the Gita dwells on only in this chapter. But even here, amidst the gloom, Krishna will not say that such a soul is eternally damned. It may be that such a sinful creature is condemned to birth after birth in harsh, unfavorable circumstances, sinking into more and more hellish states of mind; but the cycle goes on, the choice to change direction is always open, and the Atman itself can never be stained.

Lust, anger, and greed are the three doors to hell that Arjuna must at all costs not enter. The person who enters will not only fail to reach life's final goal, but will not achieve any measure of lasting happiness and prosperity.

In Sanskrit this chapter is called the "Way of Divine and Demonic Destinies." The words *deva,* god, and *asura,* demon, are not to be taken too literally here. The Hindu scriptures often tell stories of the battles between the gods and the demons; thus they dramatize the struggle between good and evil in the world. No divine character from Hindu myth escapes a challenge from some demon. Usually the god or goddess is victorious; but often the demon will win a battle or two, though not the final victory. Krishna has a long battle record, celebrated by epithets like Madhusudana, "slayer of the demon Madhu." Rama, another incarnation of Vishnu, had to confront and kill Ravana. The stories go on. The gods never seem to rest for long: there is always a new challenge to their authority, a new source of malignant evil to be destroyed.

The *Mahabharata* and the Gita do not dwell on these mythical battles. Here the interest is more frankly human, and when Krishna discusses the "divine" and "demonic" qualities, he speaks not of gods and demons but of human good and evil.

– D.M.

16 ❖ *Two Paths*

KRISHNA

[1] Be fearless and pure; never waver in your determination or your dedication to the spiritual life. Give freely. Be self-controlled, sincere, truthful, loving, and full of the desire to serve. Realize the truth of the scriptures; learn to be detached and to take joy in renunciation. [2] Do not get angry or harm any living creature, but be compassionate and gentle; show good will to all. [3] Cultivate vigor, patience, will, purity; avoid malice and pride. Then, Arjuna, you will achieve your divine destiny.

[4] Other qualities, Arjuna, make a person more and more inhuman: hypocrisy, arrogance, conceit, anger, cruelty, ignorance.

[5] The divine qualities lead to freedom; the demonic, to bondage. But do not grieve, Arjuna; you were born with divine attributes.

⁶Some people have divine tendencies, others
demonic. I have described the divine at length,
Arjuna; now listen while I describe the demonic.

⁷The demonic do things they should avoid and
avoid the things they should do. They have
no sense of uprightness, purity, or truth.

⁸"There is no God," they say, "no truth, no spiritual
law, no moral order. The basis of life is sex; what else
can it be?" ⁹Holding such distorted views, possessing
scant discrimination, they become enemies of
the world, causing suffering and destruction.

¹⁰Hypocritical, proud, and arrogant, living in
delusion and clinging to deluded ideas, insatiable
in their desires, they pursue their unclean ends.
¹¹Although burdened with fears that end only with
death, they still maintain with complete assurance,
"Gratification of lust is the highest that life can offer."

¹²Bound on all sides by scheming and anxiety, driven
by anger and greed, they amass by any means they can
a hoard of money for the satisfaction of their cravings.

¹³"I got this today," they say; "tomorrow I shall get that. This wealth is mine, and that will be mine too. ¹⁴I have destroyed my enemies. I shall destroy others too! Am I not like God? I enjoy what I want. I am successful. I am powerful. I am happy. ¹⁵I am rich and well-born. Who is equal to me? I will perform sacrifices and give gifts, and rejoice in my own generosity." This is how they go on, deluded by ignorance. ¹⁶Bound by their greed and entangled in a web of delusion, whirled about by a fragmented mind, they fall into a dark hell.

¹⁷Self-important, obstinate, swept away by the pride of wealth, they ostentatiously perform sacrifices without any regard for their purpose. ¹⁸Egotistical, violent, arrogant, lustful, angry, envious of everyone, they abuse my presence within their own bodies and in the bodies of others.

¹⁹Life after life I cast those who are malicious, hateful, cruel, and degraded into the wombs of those with similar demonic natures. ²⁰Birth after birth they find themselves with demonic tendencies. Degraded in this way, Arjuna, they fail to reach me and fall lower still.

²¹There are three gates to this self-destructive hell: lust, anger, and greed. Renounce these three.

²²Those who escape from these three gates of darkness, Arjuna, seek what is best and attain life's supreme goal. ²³Others disregard the teachings of the scriptures. Driven by selfish desire, they miss the goal of life, miss even happiness and success.

²⁴Therefore let the scriptures be your guide in what to do and what not to do. Understand their teachings; then act in accordance with them.

CHAPTER SEVENTEEN

0: *The Power of Faith*

AT THE END of the last chapter, Krishna told Arjuna to look to the scriptures to guide his actions, so that he can avoid the lower road that leads backwards to a less evolved state. Now Arjuna wants to know about those who do not follow the orthodox way set down in the scriptures, but who nevertheless offer some kind of worship with faith in their hearts.

In reply Krishna goes into greater detail about the three gunas – sattva, rajas, and tamas. He also stresses the importance of *shraddha* or faith. This is a difficult word. "Faith" is not an adequate translation, and the etymology of the word is obscure; it probably has an underlying meaning of "what is held in the heart." We might say that our shraddha is the sum total of our values, what we really hold to be important in our lives. Every human being, Krishna says, is *shraddhamaya*, "made up of faith" – as the Bible puts it, as we think in our heart, so we are.

Here, as elsewhere in the Gita, shraddha is a positive quality. It is good to have faith; yet faith can be of different kinds, different qualities. Sattvic faith is the most evolved, the most pure. Rajasic faith is dynamic, evolving, yet tainted with selfish motives. Tamasic faith goes astray in a spiritual desert.

To illustrate this, Krishna tells Arjuna that sattvic people worship the devas – the gods of heaven, of light. The rajasic worship *yakshas* and *rakshasas*. The yakshas are servants of the god of wealth; rakshasas are powerful, fearsome spirits driven by the lust for power and pleasure. Finally, tamasic people worship the spirits of the dead and ghosts.

In a practical digression, Krishna describes the different kinds of food liked by the sattvic, the rajasic, and the tamasic. Then he applies the three gunas to the act of worship and sacrifice or selfless service (*yajna*).

Verses 14–16 turn to the important question of *tapas* or *sadhana*, the disciplines undergone for the sake of spiritual growth. The Gita holds that no lasting progress is possible on the spiritual path without self-discipline. The root of the word *tapas* is *tap*, to be hot or to suffer pain; and in fact *tapas* can also mean heat or suffering. When certain spiritual practices are mastered, they create a feeling of heat in the body, which is a sign of increased spiritual potency. Tapas also refers to the power gained through spiritual austerity. Krishna dispels the mistaken belief that tapas means mortifying or torturing the body, and points out that spiritual disciplines can be sattvic, rajasic, or tamasic. The sattvic kind of tapas is offered for a truly spiritual goal; rajasic tapas is performed to gain a selfish end, probably the admiration of others. Deluded by tamas, a person will undergo painful, foolish practices to try to gain power over, or even to injure, others.

Changing course for a moment, Krishna discusses the mantram *Om Tat Sat. Om* is the most ancient of Hindu mantrams; it is the sacred syllable that is Brahman, the cosmic sound heard in the depths of meditation. *Tat* is "That," the supreme reality beyond what language can describe or thought can think. And *sat* means both "that which is" and "that which is good." The mantram *Om Tat Sat* affirms that only the good really exists; the opposite word, *asat*, implies that evil is transient and therefore is not ultimately real.

The last verse concludes that no act or intention can add to spiritual growth if it is "faithless." An act done without shraddha is *asat*, unreal; it cannot have meaning either in this world or the next.

– D.M.

17 ⫶ *The Power of Faith*

¹ O Krishna, what is the state of those who
disregard the scriptures but still worship with
faith? Do they act from sattva, rajas, or tamas?

KRISHNA

² Every creature is born with faith of some
kind, either sattvic, rajasic, or tamasic.
Listen, and I will describe each to you.

³ Our faith conforms to our nature,
Arjuna. Human nature is made of faith.
A person is what his shraddha is.

⁴ Those who are sattvic worship the forms of God;
those who are rajasic worship power and wealth.
Those who are tamasic worship spirits and ghosts.
⁵ Some invent harsh penances. Motivated by hypocrisy
and egotism, ⁶ they torture their innocent bodies and

me who dwells within. Blinded by their strength
and passion, they act and think like demons.

⁷ The three kinds of faith express themselves
in the habits of those who hold them: in the
food they like, the work they do, the disciplines
they practice, the gifts they give. Listen, and
I will describe their different ways.

⁸ Sattvic people enjoy food that is mild, tasty,
substantial, agreeable, and nourishing, food that
promotes health, strength, cheerfulness, and
longevity. ⁹ Rajasic people like food that is salty
or bitter, hot, sour, or spicy – food that promotes
pain, discomfort, and disease. ¹⁰ Tamasic people
like overcooked, stale, leftover, and impure food,
food that has lost its taste and nutritional value.

¹¹ The sattvic perform sacrifices with their entire
mind fixed on the purpose of the sacrifice. Without
thought of reward, they follow the teachings of the
scriptures. ¹² The rajasic perform sacrifices for the
sake of show and the good it will bring them. ¹³ The
tamasic perform sacrifices ignoring both the letter and
the spirit. They omit the proper prayers, the proper
offerings, the proper food, and the proper faith.

¹⁴To offer service to the gods, to the good, to the wise, and to your spiritual teacher; purity, honesty, continence, and nonviolence: these are the disciplines of the body. ¹⁵To offer soothing words, to speak truly, kindly, and helpfully, and to study the scriptures: these are the disciplines of speech. ¹⁶Calmness, gentleness, silence, self-restraint, and purity: these are the disciplines of the mind.

¹⁷When these three levels of self-discipline are practiced without attachment to the results, but in a spirit of great faith, the sages call this practice sattvic. ¹⁸Disciplines practiced in order to gain respect, honor, or admiration are rajasic; they are undependable and transitory in their effects. ¹⁹Disciplines practiced to gain power over others, or in the confused belief that to torture oneself is spiritual, are tamasic.

²⁰Giving simply because it is right to give, without thought of return, at a proper time, in proper circumstances, and to a worthy person, is sattvic giving. ²¹Giving with regrets or in the expectation of receiving some favor or of getting something in return is rajasic. ²²Giving at an inappropriate time, in inappropriate circumstances, and to an unworthy person, without affection or respect, is tamasic.

²³*Om Tat Sat*: these three words represent Brahman, from which come priests and scriptures and sacrifice. ²⁴Those who follow the Vedas, therefore, always repeat the word *Om* when offering sacrifices, performing spiritual disciplines, or giving gifts. ²⁵Those seeking liberation and not any personal benefit add the word *Tat* when performing these acts of worship, discipline, and charity. ²⁶*Sat* means "that which is"; it also indicates goodness. Therefore it is used to describe a worthy deed.

²⁷To be steadfast in self-sacrifice, self-discipline, and giving is *sat*. To act in accordance with these three is *sat* as well. ²⁸But to engage in sacrifice, self-discipline, and giving without good faith is *asat,* without worth or goodness, either in this life or in the next.

▣ *Freedom & Renunciation*

THIS FINAL CHAPTER of the Gita roams over many subjects, beginning with a discussion of the merits of renunciation versus the life of personally involved action. To begin with, Arjuna asks about two words commonly used for renunciation in Sanskrit, *sannyasa* and *tyaga*. Both words come from roots meaning to give up or abandon. *Sannyasa* acquired the specialized meaning of giving up ordinary life to live the austere, wandering life of a homeless pilgrim. A *sannyasi* is a monk: one who does not participate in family life and has withdrawn from society. In a sense, he has withdrawn from life. Krishna does not recommend this kind of renunciation. In fact, he says it is impossible for anyone to "give up" in this way, for as long as we have a body, we have to do a certain amount of work just to maintain it. Krishna does not advise dropping out of life, and the Gita is primarily aimed at people who live "in the world" yet desire genuine spiritual fulfillment.

The kind of renunciation Krishna recommends is *tyaga*,

where it is not activity but selfish desire for the rewards of action – of work, of life – that is to be renounced. Arjuna is advised to fulfill all his responsibilities, but without a selfish motive. In particular, he should not give up the three great virtuous works – sacrifice, giving, and spiritual disciplines.

Having made plain to Arjuna that renunciation is essential, Krishna goes on to explain that renunciation can be of three kinds, depending upon the guna that dominates the individual's personality. As may be expected, rajasic and tamasic renunciation leave something to be desired.

Many times Krishna has said that renunciation of the fruits of work is essential. Perhaps the verse in chapter 2 said it best – that we have control over our work and actions, but we have no command of the results. The word *karma-phala-tyaga* appears again and again, and the literal translation is "renunciation of the fruits of action." In this final chapter, literally "The Freedom [moksha] That Comes from Renunciation," Krishna sums up his teaching that in work, in life, one must not be driven by a selfish desire for any kind of reward, for such compulsive work can only stunt full spiritual development. In addition, Krishna points out, when we act out of selfish attachment, we must fully partake of the result, the karma, of every thought, word, and deed; and although these results may be what was desired, they may also be something not desired at all, or a little of both (18:12). In this life we can never be sure that things will turn out as planned.

In verse 13 the Sankhya philosophy is again mentioned. Scholars believe that at the time the Gita was composed the Sankhya school was at an early stage of development, yet even here we see the characteristic method of thorough categorizing. Using the Sankhya categories of the three gunas, the Gita goes on to give more detail about work, which is of three kinds – sattvic, rajasic, and tamasic. Similarly, the doer of the work is shown to be dominated by one of these all-pervasive qualities. In a very interesting passage Krishna talks of three kinds of happiness – a practical application of the abstract theories of Sankhya (18:36–39).

Pursuing the world of work, and how it contributes to spiritual growth, the Gita gives a short explanation of caste in this chapter. The Gita is not especially interested in caste – the social hierarchy of Hindu society – but we do find a short explanation here. The *sannyasi,* the renouncing monk, has left society and therefore belongs to no caste, but Krishna does not point out that course to Arjuna. Rather, he wants Arjuna to lead an active life. Krishna tells him that devotion to his own duty is best. It is better to do one's own work, even if imperfectly, than to try to take on some other work. The work proper to each of the four castes is then described. In general, the Gita takes a liberal view of caste, and it would be wrong to interpret this chapter as supporting a rigid caste system.

The final part of this chapter, verses 50 and following, give a picture of the person who has attained *siddhi*– success or perfection – in the spiritual life and who goes on to union with Brahman.

In verse 61 Krishna returns to a favorite topic – the Lord dwelling in the hearts of all beings. But here he adds a startling revelation: the Lord dwells in all, yet he "whirls them around" through maya as if they were toys mounted on a machine. Having jarred Arjuna with this amazing image, Krishna reassures him that he can escape from the machine, the wheel of time, through devotion to God. If he wholeheartedly takes refuge in the Lord within, then through Krishna's grace he will find peace.

As his all but final word, Krishna reminds Arjuna that he holds him very dear. Through devotion, Arjuna will be able to find his way, and he should not forget that Krishna feels deep love for him.

The relationship between the teacher and student is given a parting word, partially of warning. Krishna does not want these profound truths told to anyone who is not ready. Anyone lacking devotion or self-control, who does not want to hear spiritual instruction or who scoffs at it, should not be accepted as a student. The sacred act of giving spiritual instruction cannot be undertaken lightly. It is the highest work, and the man or woman who does it is most dear to Krishna.

Finally, Krishna asks Arjuna if he has understood. Arjuna says yes, his conflicts are over; he is ready to follow Krishna's instructions. This concludes the dialogue between Krishna and Arjuna and the instruction of the Gita proper. Sanjaya, who has been narrating the poem to blind king Dhritarash-tra, adds a few final verses of benediction. He has "seen" this dialogue through his mystic vision, granted by the grace of Vyasa. Just recalling this wonderful conversation makes his hair stand on end in ecstasy, and when he remembers Krishna's wonderful beauty, his joy is boundless.

– D.M.

18 ❧ *Freedom & Renunciation*

ARJUNA

¹O Krishna, destroyer of evil, please explain
to me *sannyasa* and *tyaga* and how one kind
of renunciation differs from another.

KRISHNA

²To refrain from selfish acts is one kind of
renunciation, called sannyasa; to renounce
the fruit of action is another, called tyaga.

³Among the wise, some say that all action should
be renounced as evil. Others say that certain
kinds of action – self-sacrifice, giving, and
self-discipline – should be continued. ⁴Listen,
Arjuna, and I will explain three kinds of tyaga
and my conclusions concerning them.

⁵Self-sacrifice, giving, and self-discipline should
not be renounced, for they purify the thoughtful.

⁶Yet even these, Arjuna, should be performed
without desire for selfish rewards. This is essential.

⁷To renounce one's responsibilities is not fitting.
The wise call such deluded renunciation tamasic.
⁸To avoid action from fear of difficulty or physical
discomfort is rajasic. There is no reward in such
renunciation. ⁹But to fulfill your responsibilities
knowing that they are obligatory, while at the same
time desiring nothing for yourself – this is sattvic
renunciation. ¹⁰Those endowed with sattva clearly
understand the meaning of renunciation and do
not waver. They are not intimidated by unpleasant
work, nor do they seek a job because it is pleasant.

¹¹As long as one has a body, one cannot renounce
action altogether. True renunciation is giving up all
desire for personal reward. ¹²Those who are attached
to personal reward will reap the consequences of
their actions: some pleasant, some unpleasant, some
mixed. But those who renounce every desire for
personal reward go beyond the reach of karma.

¹³Listen, Arjuna, and I will explain the five elements
necessary for the accomplishment of every action,
as taught by the wisdom of Sankhya. ¹⁴The body,

the means, the ego, the performance of the act,
and the divine will: ¹⁵these are the five factors in all
actions, right or wrong, in thought, word, or deed.

¹⁶Those who do not understand this think of
themselves as separate agents. With their crude
intellects they fail to see the truth. ¹⁷The person
who is free from ego, who has attained purity
of heart, though he slays these people, he does
not slay and is not bound by his action.

¹⁸Knowledge, the thing to be known, and the
knower: these three promote action. The means,
the act itself, and the doer: these three are the
totality of action. ¹⁹Knowledge, action, and the doer
can be described according to the gunas. Listen,
and I will explain their distinctions to you.

²⁰Sattvic knowledge sees the one indestructible Being
in all beings, the unity underlying the multiplicity
of creation. ²¹Rajasic knowledge sees all things
and creatures as separate and distinct. ²²Tamasic
knowledge, lacking any sense of perspective, sees
one small part and mistakes it for the whole.

[23]Work performed to fulfill one's obligations, without thought of personal reward or of whether the job is pleasant or unpleasant, is sattvic. [24]Work prompted by selfish desire or self-will, full of stress, is rajasic. [25]Work that is undertaken blindly, without any consideration of consequences, waste, injury to others, or one's own capacities, is tamasic.

[26]Sattvic workers are free from egotism and selfish attachments, full of enthusiasm and fortitude in success and failure alike. [27]Rajasic workers have strong personal desires and crave rewards for their actions. Covetous, impure, and destructive, they are easily swept away by fortune, good or bad. [28]Tamasic workers are undisciplined, vulgar, stubborn, deceitful, dishonest, and lazy. They are easily depressed and prone to procrastination.

[29]Listen, Arjuna, as I describe the three types of understanding and will.

[30]To know when to act and when to refrain from action, what is right action and what is wrong, what brings security and what insecurity, what brings freedom and what bondage: these are the signs of a sattvic intellect.

³¹The rajasic intellect confuses right and wrong actions, and cannot distinguish what is to be done from what should not be done. ³²The tamasic intellect is shrouded in darkness, utterly reversing right and wrong wherever it turns.

³³The sattvic will, developed through meditation, keeps prana, mind, and senses in vital harmony. ³⁴The rajasic will, conditioned by selfish desire, pursues wealth, pleasure, and respectability. ³⁵The tamasic will shows itself in obstinate ignorance, sloth, fear, grief, depression, and conceit.

³⁶Now listen, Arjuna: there are also three kinds of happiness. By sustained effort, one comes to the end of sorrow. ³⁷That which seems like poison at first, but tastes like nectar in the end – this is the joy of sattva, born of a mind at peace with itself. ³⁸Pleasure from the senses seems like nectar at first, but it is bitter as poison in the end. This is the kind of happiness that comes to the rajasic. ³⁹Those who are tamasic draw their pleasures from sleep, indolence, and intoxication. Both in the beginning and in the end, this happiness is a delusion.

⁴⁰No creature, whether born on earth or among
the gods in heaven, is free from the conditioning
of the three gunas. ⁴¹The different responsibilities
found in the social order – distinguishing
brahmin, kshatriya, vaishya, and shudra
– have their roots in this conditioning.

⁴²The responsibilities to which brahmins are
born, based on their nature, are self-control,
tranquility, purity of heart, patience, humility,
learning, austerity, wisdom, and faith.

⁴³The qualities of kshatriyas, based on their
nature, are courage, strength, fortitude, dexterity,
generosity, leadership, and the firm resolve never
to retreat from battle. ⁴⁴The occupations suitable
for a vaishya are agriculture, dairying, and trade.
The proper work of a shudra is service.

⁴⁵By devotion to one's own particular duty,
everyone can attain perfection. Let me tell you how.
⁴⁶By performing one's own work, one worships
the Creator who dwells in every creature. Such
worship brings that person to fulfillment.

⁴⁷It is better to perform one's own duties
imperfectly than to master the duties of another.
By fulfilling the obligations he is born with, a
person never comes to grief. ⁴⁸No one should
abandon duties because he sees defects in them.
Every action, every activity, is surrounded by
defects as a fire is surrounded by smoke.

⁴⁹One who is free from selfish attachments, who
has mastered himself and his passions, attains
the supreme perfection of freedom from action.
⁵⁰Listen and I shall explain now, Arjuna, how one
who has attained perfection also attains Brahman,
the supreme consummation of wisdom.

⁵¹Unerring in discrimination, sovereign of
the senses and passions, free from the clamor
of likes and dislikes, ⁵²such a one leads a
simple, self-reliant life based on meditation,
controlling speech, body, and mind.

⁵³Free from self-will, aggressiveness, arrogance, anger,
and the lust to possess people or things, they are at
peace with themselves and others and enter into the
unitive state. ⁵⁴United with Brahman, ever joyful,
beyond the reach of desire and sorrow, they have equal

regard for every living creature and attain supreme devotion to me. ⁵⁵By loving me they come to know me truly; then they know my glory and enter into my boundless being. ⁵⁶All their acts are performed in my service, and through my grace they win eternal life.

⁵⁷Make every act an offering to me; regard me as your only protector. Relying on interior discipline, meditate on me always. ⁵⁸Remembering me, you shall overcome all difficulties through my grace. But if you will not heed me in your self-will, nothing will avail you.

⁵⁹If you egotistically say, "I will not fight this battle," your resolve will be useless; your own nature will drive you into it. ⁶⁰Your own karma, born of your own nature, will drive you to do even that which you do not wish to do, because of your delusion.

⁶¹The Lord dwells in the hearts of all creatures and whirls them round upon the wheel of maya. ⁶²Run to him for refuge with all your strength, and peace profound will be yours through his grace.

⁶³I give you these precious words of wisdom; reflect on them and then do as you choose. ⁶⁴These are the

last words I shall speak to you, dear one, for your
spiritual fulfillment. You are very dear to me.

⁶⁵Be aware of me always, adore me, make every
act an offering to me, and you shall come to me;
this I promise; for you are dear to me. ⁶⁶Abandon
all supports and look to me for protection. I shall
purify you from the sins of the past; do not grieve.

⁶⁷Do not share this wisdom with anyone who lacks
in devotion or self-control, lacks the desire to learn,
or scoffs at me. ⁶⁸Those who teach this supreme
mystery of the Gita to all who love me perform the
greatest act of love; they will come to me without
doubt. ⁶⁹No one can render me more devoted
service; no one on earth can be more dear to me.

⁷⁰Those who meditate on these holy words worship
me with wisdom and devotion. ⁷¹Even those who
listen to them with faith, free from doubts, will
find a happier world where good people dwell.

⁷²Have you listened with attention? Are you
now free from your doubts and confusion?

ARJUNA

[73]You have dispelled my doubts and delusions,
and I understand through your grace. My
faith is firm now, and I will do your will.

SANJAYA

[74]This is the dialogue I heard between Krishna,
the son of Vasudeva, and Arjuna, the great-
hearted son of Pritha. The wonder of it makes
my hair stand on end! [75]Through Vyasa's grace, I
have heard the supreme secret of spiritual union
directly from the Lord of Yoga, Krishna himself.

[76]Whenever I remember these wonderful, holy words
between Krishna and Arjuna, I am filled with joy.
[77]And when I remember the breathtaking form of
Krishna, I am filled with wonder and my joy overflows.

[78]Wherever the divine Krishna and the mighty
Arjuna are, there will be prosperity, victory,
happiness, and sound judgment. Of this I am sure!

◫ *Notes*

CHAPTER ONE

1 The phrase "on the field of dharma" (*dharma-kshetre*) gives a hint that the battle is to be an allegorical one, a fight of dharma, justice, against adharma, evil. The battle takes place not only at Kurukshetra, the "field of the Kurus," but also on the elusive "field of dharma," the spiritual realm where all moral struggles are waged.

40–44 These verses are particularly difficult to translate, because they revolve around the complex word *dharma*: law, justice, or simply something's inner nature. To try to capture the word in English we might say "God's law" or "eternal truth." Dharma is divinely given; it is the force that holds things together in a unity, the center that must hold if all is to go well. The opposite of dharma is *adharma*: evil, injustice, chaos. In these verses Arjuna gives expression to his fears of a coming chaos, an evil world where good people will be confused and violated. "Sense of unity" here translates *dharma*; the phrase "loses its sense of unity" would be more literally translated as "is overcome by *adharma*."

The translation speaks in a general way of the chaos that overcomes society when dharma is weak – when ancient spiritual truths are ignored. Thus *varna-samkara,* literally "confusion of caste," is more meaningful as "society [is] plunged into chaos." The subject here is not the observance of caste restrictions, but the essential cohesion of the social fabric.

42 The Sanskrit refers to the ancient *pinda* rites that offer homage to dead ancestors. These rites maintained the traditions of the family by respecting and worshipping those who had gone before. Again, the rather liberal rendering "the spiritual evolution begun by our ancestors" seems preferable to a narrower translation.

CHAPTER TWO

17 *Tat,* "that," is an ancient name for Brahman, the supreme reality. Brahman is neither masculine nor feminine; in fact, it has no attributes at all. It is impossible to describe Brahman in words, so it is simply pointed to: *tat.*

72 The state of immortality is *brahma-nirvana,* "the nirvana that is Brahman." This is the state of release or liberation, union with the divine ground of existence. The word *nirvana* comes from the Sanskrit root *va* "to blow" with the prefix *nir* "out"; it means "to extinguish," as a fire is said to be "blown out." Thus it indicates the extinction of the old, limited personality. By adding the word *brahman,* complete union with the universal Godhead is indicated. *Brahma-nirvana* then means the mystic state of extinction of self in the union with God. *Nirvana* is a Buddhist term as well. Some misconceptions are unfortunately current about this rather esoteric concept. Nirvana is wrongly presented as a kind of empty nothingness, even a spiritual death. We get exactly the opposite impression if we approach the Hindus and Buddhists themselves. It is true there is much talk of extinguishing the petty ego and going beyond self-will – the mask that

hides the creative, wise, loving Self underneath. This "death" of the old person to make way for the new is one purpose of spiritual disciplines. It can be painful, but the death of the old does not lead to annihilation but to a spiritual rebirth.

CHAPTER THREE

9 Here and later *yajna* is translated as "selfless work" or "selfless service." The literal meaning is sacrifice: essentially, self-sacrifice, giving up something one greatly values for the sake of a higher purpose. Some translators give a very narrow translation of *yajna* as a ritualistic sacrifice, but this is inaccurate.

39 *Kama* can be translated as selfish desire or pleasure, and often carries a connotation of sensual desire or sexual passion. It means essentially a personal desire for ease or pleasure, not "desire" of a more altruistic kind.

CHAPTER FOUR

37 This is a well-known verse. The meanings of *karma* are complex, but the verse is widely taken to mean that true knowledge destroys the effects of past errors, which generate further karma. When consciousness is unified and illumined, one is released from the bondage of karma.

CHAPTER FIVE

6 *Yoga* has many meanings in the Gita. Here *yoga* is translated as "action" and "selfless service" because a contrast is being made between Sankhya and yoga: that is, between philosophical explanation and the actual practice of the spiritual life.

9 The word for "senses" in Sanskrit is *indriya*, literally "faculty" or "power." The indriyas are not only the five faculties of perception (seeing, hearing, touching, smelling, and tasting) but also

those of action, whose organs are the hands, the feet, the tongue, and the organs of excretion and reproduction.

13 "The city of nine gates" is the body. The gates are the two eyes, the two nostrils, the two ears, the mouth, and the organs of excretion and reproduction. In some lists these gates are expanded to eleven by adding the navel and the *brahmarandhra* or sagittal suture, the opening at the top of the skull.

27–28 The area "of spiritual consciousness" between the eyebrows is one of the seven centers of awareness or *chakras* described in yoga literature. These seven chakras, though not physical, are said to lie along a channel for awakened spiritual energy (*kundalini*) that corresponds with the spine; the chakras are located at the level of the anus, sex organs, stomach, heart, throat, eyebrows, and the top of the head. Kundalini circulates among these centers, but it is usually confined to the lowest three chakras, corresponding to the main preoccupations of life on the physical level. In yogic concentration the vital energy (kundalini) rises; samadhi is said to take place when it reaches the chakras at the brow or head.

CHAPTER SIX

11 This describes the traditional seat used for meditation. The Gita is not concerned with the outer forms of the spiritual life, but here we do get a mention of the grass and deerskin used by the ancient sages. Perhaps the point is that they used what was available in their forest retreats, and that the seat should be what Patanjali calls *sukhasana*: comfortable enough to forget about your body.

14 "All actions dedicated to Brahman" is a literal translation of the

Sanskrit word *brahmacharya,* a life of self-control and sense restraint.

CHAPTER SEVEN

16 *Artharthi* has given translators some difficulties. "Those who desire to achieve their purpose" captures the basic meaning of the word. *Artha* is goal or purpose; the second word of the compound, *arthi,* means "one who has a goal." So *artharthi* probably refers to those who take to the spiritual life with a particular purpose in view. *Artha* also means wealth or worldly goods, but to translate this phrase as "those who desire wealth" would go against the entire tenor of the Gita.

23 "The gods" here are the *devas,* the lower, celestial deities such as Indra.

30 These obscure terms (*adhibhuta, adhidaiva,* and *adhiyajna*) are taken up in the next chapter.

CHAPTER EIGHT

6 Whatever is the content of the mind at the moment of death determines the direction of the soul's rebirth. The implication is that whatever has been the bedrock of consciousness during life will be remembered at the time of death and lead the soul on to fulfill that desire in the next life.

9–10 The eyebrow center is discussed in the note to 5:27–28.

CHAPTER NINE

5 *Yoga* here means "mysterious power." This is yet another meaning attached to the word *yoga,* for those who practiced *yoga* were sometimes thought of as concealing within themselves extraordinary powers developed through their disciplines. The folklore

of India relates many stories about mysterious yogis who have strange, divine powers.

Krishna speaks here of his *yoga aishvaram,* his mysterious and majestic power. *Ishvara* means "lord" and *aishvaram* "lordly": Krishna's yoga is something he uses as Ishvara, the Lord of the world. Now he begins to show Arjuna something of the nature of the mystery.

17 Rig, Yajur, and Sama are the principal Vedas, the ancient scriptures that are Hinduism's orthodox authority.

20–21 These verses repeat the idea that heaven itself is an impermanent state. After exhausting the store of their good karma, the blessed souls in heaven must be reborn on earth. Only the liberated soul, the one who has found union with Krishna or *brahmanirvana,* escapes the round of rebirth and death as a separate, mortal creature.

CHAPTER TEN

This chapter contains many Sanskrit names, which are briefly identified in the glossary (see p. 279).

18 *Amrita,* "immortal," comes from *a* "not" and *mrita* "mortal." The Greek word *ambrosia* is cognate and has the same meanings: amrita is the *ambrosia* of the gods, the drink that makes them live forever, and in a general sense it means sweet or nectar-like. So the translation could also be "your words, which are like ambrosia."

22 The mind (*manas*) is here taken to be one of the senses or indriyas of perception; for example, it is really with the mind rather than with the eye that we see.

33 The Sanskrit alphabet, too, begins with the letter *a*; perhaps this is why Krishna declares that among letters he is *a,* the first. Another possible reason is that *a* is the most frequent sound in Sanskrit.

CHAPTER ELEVEN

14 Here Arjuna presses the palms of his hands together in the gesture called *anjali,* like the Western gesture of prayer. This is the usual form of respectful greeting in India, as well as being used in worship and prayer.

15 Brahma, the Creator (not to be confused with Brahman, the attributeless Godhead, which is beyond the Trinity of creation, preservation, and destruction) sits within a lotus that grows from the navel of Lord Vishnu.

17 Here Arjuna sees not his friend Krishna, but the Lord incarnate in Krishna: Vishnu, armed with his traditional weapons, a club (or mace) and a discus. Not mentioned in this verse are the two benign symbols he carries in his other hands, a conch and a lotus.

CHAPTER TWELVE

1 Arjuna is asking which path is superior, that of knowledge (jnana yoga) or love (bhakti yoga).

CHAPTER THIRTEEN

5 This is a list of all the twenty-four categories given in Sankhya philosophy to describe phenomena in the field of prakriti.

CHAPTER FIFTEEN

1 The *ashvattha* is the sacred pipal tree, a kind of fig often grown in temple compounds in India. The idea of a "world tree" appears

in many ancient cultures. Here the Gita uses the image of the tree as "upside down," drawing on the fact that the pipal sends out aerial roots, making "branches above and below." The image illustrates the phenomenal world, rooted in Brahman, complete unity, and branching out into the apparent diversity of life.

13 *Rasatmaka soma* is here translated as "life-giving fluid," the nourishment of plants. In Hindu mythology it is the moon, sometimes called Soma, that nourishes plants, as the source of the life-giving nectar called Soma. In the Vedas, soma is an intoxicating, invigorating drink distilled from a plant grown high in the mountains and drunk by participants in a sacred ritual. Scholars have tried to discover what the soma plant might have been, but so far no conclusive identification has been made. Soma also appears as an important god in the Vedas.

CHAPTER SEVENTEEN

27–28 *Sat* means that which is real or true and that which is good; it derives from the Sanskrit verb *as,* to be, and is directly related to our English word *is.* It is noteworthy that this word *sat* links reality and goodness, reflecting the idea that good is eternal; it is merely covered from time to time by *asat,* evil, which is temporary and in that sense unreal. *Asat* is formed from *sat* by the addition of the prefix *a* "without," very much the way English forms words like *amoral.*

CHAPTER EIGHTEEN

1 *Sannyasa* and *tyaga* both mean renunciation, *sannyasa* from the root *as* "to cast aside" and *tyaga* from *tyaj* "to give up." The distinction between these two is clarified in the introduction to this chapter.

14 "The divine will" is a translation of *daivam,* which comes from

the word *deva,* "god." *Daivam* is sometimes translated as "fate," but this is inappropriate in the Gita, which is not at all fatalistic. The Gita does, however, allow a place for God's will or Providence in the affairs of humankind – though of course the dominant force is usually karma, not daivam.

34 This verse uses the phrase *dharma-kama-artha,* "duty, pleasure, and wealth," traditionally considered the three goals of ordinary human life. The fourth and highest goal is *moksha,* salvation. The rajasic personality, as this verse points out, pursues the first three worldly goals; moksha is ignored.

41 The Vedas establish the fourfold division of society into the classes of brahmin, kshatriya, vaishya, and shudra – roughly priests and intellectuals; warriors and rulers; businessmen, farmers, and craftsmen; and workers and servants.

66 *Dharma* is not used here in the usual sense of law or inner nature, but in a rarer meaning: a thing's attribute, condition, or conditioning. Usually *dharma* is used in this sense only in the plural, as here: thus dharma is divine law; dharmas are the innumerable beings, things, emotions and mental states that make up everyday existence as we experience it. Here, following the root meaning (*dhri,* to support or hold up), *sarva-dharman* is translated as "all your supports," in the sense of external props, conditioned dependencies. Another translation would be: "Cast off your dependency on everything external, Arjuna, and rely on the Self alone."

◫ *Glossary*

THIS BRIEF GLOSSARY is a guide only to Sanskrit terms used in this volume. Words used once and explained in context are not included. As a rough guide, Sanskrit vowels may be pronounced as in Italian or Spanish. The combinations *kh, gh, th, dh, ph,* and *bh* are always pronounced as the consonant plus a slight *h* sound: *th* as in hot*h*ead (not as in *th*ing); *ph* as in ha*ph*azard (not as in *ph*one).

Every Sanskrit vowel has a short and a long form, the long pronounced for twice as long as the short. The diphthongs – e, ai, o, au – are also long. To simplify the spelling of Sanskrit words in this glossary we have retained only the long mark (ˉ) for the long vowels, omitting the other diacritics sometimes used to spell Sanskrit words in English.

adharma "Not dharma." Injustice, evil, anything which goes against moral laws.

advaita Having no duality; the supreme Reality, which is the "One without a second." The word *advaita* is especially used in Vedanta philosophy, which stresses the unity of the Self (Ātman) and Brahman.

ahamkāra [*aham* "I"; *kāra* "maker"] Self-will, separateness.

ahimsā [*a* "not"; *himsā* "violence"] Nonviolence, doing no injury, wishing no harm.

ākāsha Space, sky; the most subtle of the five elements.

akshara The eternal; the syllable *Om*.

Ananta The cosmic serpent on which Vishnu reclines in rest.

apara ["not transcendent"] Lower knowledge; intellectual knowledge.

Arjuna One of the five Pāndava brothers and an important figure in Indian epic and legend. He is Srī Krishna's beloved disciple and friend in the Bhagavad Gītā.

Aryaman "The noble one," a Vedic god, revered as an ancestor of mankind.

asat [*a* "not"; *sat* "truth, goodness"] Untruth; anything unreal, untrue, or lacking in goodness.

ashvattha The pipal tree, a kind of fig; it is regarded as holy and often grows in temple compounds.

Ashvatthāma A great archer and warrior who is Drona's son.

asura In Hindu myth, a demon; figuratively, a being with an evil nature.

Ātman "Self"; the innermost soul in every creature, which is divine.

avatāra [*ava* "down"; *tri* "to cross"] The descent of God to earth; the incarnation of Vishnu on earth; the birth of divine consciousness in the human heart.

avidyā [*a* "not"; *vidyā* "wisdom"] Ignorance, lack of wisdom, want of knowledge.

avyaya The eternal, the changeless.

Bhagavad Gītā [*Bhagavat* "lord"; *gītā* "song"] "The Song of the
     Lord," name of a Hindu scripture which contains the
     instructions of Srī Krishna.

bhakti Devotion, worship, love.

bhakti yoga The Way of Love.

Bhīshma A revered elder of the Kaurava dynasty who allows
     himself to be killed by Arjuna in the *Mahābhārata*
     battle.

Bhrigu A sage famous in ancient legend.

Brahmā God as creator, one of the Hindu Trinity; the others
     are Vishnu, the Preserver, and Shiva, the Destroyer.
     Brahmā should not be confused with *Brahman*.
     (See entry below.)

brahmacharya "Conduct leading to God," self-control, purity.

Brahman The supreme reality underlying all life, the divine ground
     of existence, the impersonal Godhead.

brahmanirvāna "Nirvana in Brahman," the final state of spiritual
     fulfillment: eternal union with Brahman, the ground of all
     being.

Brahmavidyā The science of knowing Brahman.

brahmin [Skt. *brāhmana*] Literally, a person who strives to know
     Brahman; in traditional Hindu society, a person of the
     priestly or learned class.

Brihaspati The guru or priest of the gods.

Buddha [from *budh* "to wake up"] "The Awakened one," the title
     given to the sage Siddhārtha Gautama Shākyamuni after
     he obtained complete illumination. The Buddha lived and
     taught in North India during the sixth century B.C.

buddhi Understanding, intelligence; the faculty of discrimination;
     correct view, idea, purpose.

Chitraratha "Having a bright chariot," the king of Gandharvas.

daivam Divine will; destiny.

deva A divine being, a god. The devas of Hindu mythology resemble the Olympians of the ancient Greeks – extraordinary, immortal, yet not unlike mortal men and women in their behavior. The feminine is *devī,* "goddess."

dharma Law, duty; the universal law which holds all life together in unity.

Dhritarāshtra The king of the Kurus. He has been blind since birth and has therefore never been enthroned as the rightful king, but he serves as de facto ruler. The entire Bhagavad Gītā is a narration told by Sanjaya to the blind king, whose sons are the Kauravas.

Draupadī The royal princess who became the wife of each of the five Pāndava brothers.

Drona A learned brahmin who became a warrior, and eventually general of the Kaurava army. The preceptor of the royal princes, he taught the heroes of the *Mahābhārata* the skills of war.

duhkha Pain, suffering, sorrow.

Duryodhana The oldest son of Dhritarāshtra and the chief enemy of the Pāndavas and Srī Krishna.

dvandva In Sanskrit grammar, a kind of compound that combines two or more words as a pair or group.

Gandharva Heavenly musicians who are demigods, rather touchy and proud, handsome and amorous.

Gāndīva Arjuna's bow, which was a gift from the god of fire.

Ganges [Skt. gangā] A major river of northern India, revered as a sacred symbol.

Garuda The great eagle that is Vishnu's vehicle.

gāyatrī A meter used in Vedic hymns; a prayer to the sun composed in this meter.

Gītā "The Song," a shorter title for the Bhagavad Gītā.

guna Quality; specifically, the three qualities which make up the
phenomenal world: *sattva*, law, harmony, purity, goodness;
rajas, energy, passion; and *tamas*, inertia, ignorance. The
corresponding adjectives are *sattvic*, *rajasic*, and *tamasic*.

guru A spiritual teacher.

Hari Name of Vishnu or Krishna.

Hastināpura "City of the elephants," an important city in ancient
India, located about sixty miles northeast of the modern
Delhi. It was the capital of the Pāndavas and their line.

Himālaya [*hima* "snow"; *ālaya* "abode"] The great mountain range
which stretches across the northern border of India, important in mythology as the home of Shiva and other gods.

Ikshvāku The son of Manu, and founder of the Solar Dynasty of
kings.

Indra The god of storms and battle. In the Veda, Indra is the chief
of the gods (devas) and an important deity; later his role is
greatly diminished.

Īshvara The Lord; God.

Janaka A king of ancient times who was both an effective ruler and
a holy sage.

Janārdana "He who stirs up the people," name of Krishna.

jīva Living being; the living soul; the finite, individual soul that is
identified with separate existence, as opposed to Ātman,
the eternal Self.

jnāna [from *jnā* "to know"] Wisdom; higher knowledge.

jnāna yoga The Way of Wisdom.

kalpa A period in cosmic time equaling one Day of Brahmā or
1,000 "great yugas" – a total of 4,320 million years. See also
yuga.

kāma Selfish desire, greed; sexual desire, sometimes personified as
Kāmadeva.

Kāmadhuk "The cow of wishes," who in legend fulfills all desires.

Kapila Name of a sage, first teacher of the Sānkhya philosophy.

karma [from *kri* "to do"] Action; former actions which will lead to
    certain results in a cause-and-effect relationship.

karma yoga The Way of Action; the path of selfless service.

Karna A brave warrior who plays an important role in the larger
    epic, but is only mentioned in passing in the Gītā.

Kauravas "The sons of Kuru," Duryodhana and his brothers, who
    are the enemies of the Pāndava brothers.

Kripa A revered teacher of the royal family who also serves as a
    warrior.

Krishna ["black"; or from *krish* "to draw, to attract to oneself"]
    "The Dark One" or "He who draws us to Himself," name
    of an incarnation of Vishnu. Vishnu, the cosmic force
    of goodness, comes to earth as Krishna to reestablish
    dharma, or law. Krishna is the friend and advisor of the
    Pāndava brothers, especially Arjuna, to whom he reveals the
    teachings of the Bhagavad Gītā. He is the inner Lord, who
    personifies spiritual love and lives in the hearts of all beings.

kshatriya A warrior or prince; a member of the ruling class of tradi-
    tional Hindu society.

kshetra A field; a place; a sacred place or temple.

Kubera God of wealth.

kundalinī "The serpent power," spiritual or evolutionary energy. In
    yoga literature, kundalinī is described as a force coiled at
    the base of the spine. Kundalinī may be aroused through
    meditation and the practice of yoga; then it rises up
    through the subtle body, awakening the higher centers of
    consciousness.

Kurukshetra "The field of the Kurus," where the *Mahābhārata* battle
    takes place. It is north of the modern city of Delhi.

līlā Game; the divine play of the Lord disguising himself as the
    many beings of this world.

Mādhava Another name for Krishna, "of the Madhava clan."

Madhusūdana "Slayer of Madhu," a name for Krishna, who killed the demon Madhu.

Mahābhārata Name of the great Indian epic composed some 2,500 years ago, traditionally attributed to the sage Vyāsa. It relates the conflict between the descendants of Pāndu (the forces of light) and those of Dhritarāshtra (the forces of darkness).

manas The mind; specifically, the faculty which registers and stores sensory impressions.

mantram [or *mantra*] A holy name or phrase; a spiritual formula.

Manu The father of the human race, the Hindu equivalent of Adam or the first man.

Mārgashīrsha The lunar month that falls in November – December.

Marīchi A Vedic demigod. The name means "particle of light."

Māyā Illusion; appearance, as contrasted with Reality; the creative power of God.

Meerā A woman saint of medieval India remembered for her songs to her beloved Krishna.

Meru A mythical mountain said to stand at the center of the world or cosmos. The gods dwell on Meru in beautiful cities, amidst flowering gardens.

moksha Liberation, salvation, illumination.

Nakula One of the junior Pāndava brothers.

Nārada The divine musician and sage who is a devotee of Sri Krishna.

Nirvāna [*nir* "out"; *vāna* "to blow"] Complete extinction of self-will and separateness; realization of the unity of all life. (See also Notes, p.268.)

nirvikalpa samādhi A state of spiritual awareness in which there is no perception of duality, of inside or outside, of subject and object; merger in the impersonal Godhead.

Om [or *Aum*] The cosmic sound, heard in deep meditation; the

Holy Word, taught in the Upanishads, which signifies Brahman, the divine ground of existence.

Pāndavas "The sons of Pāndu," a collective name for Arjuna and his four brothers, Yudhishthira, Bhīma, Nakula, and Sahadeva. The Pāndavas are in conflict with the Kauravas; both claim the ancient throne of Hastināpura. The Gītā is placed on the eve of the battle that will decide this conflict. The Pāndavas are looked upon as the forces for good and the Kauravas as wicked usurpers.

Pārtha "Son of Prithā," a name for Arjuna – or for his brothers Bhīma and Yudhishthira.

Patanjali The author of the *Yoga Sūtras*, a classic description of the way to Self-realization through meditation. Patanjali lived around the second century B.C., and his method is sometimes referred to as *rāja yoga*.

Pāvaka "The purifier," a name for the god of fire.

Prahlāda A demon prince who was greatly devoted to Vishnu.

Prajāpati "Lord of offspring," the creator of all beings. Indian myth encompasses many creation stories, and sometimes one great Father, or Prajāpati, is mentioned; sometimes there are seven or more fathers or sages who created all living creatures.

prajnā [from *jnā* "to know"] A transcendental mode of knowing developed in deep meditation.

prakriti The basic energy from which the mental and physical worlds take shape; nature.

prāna Breath; vital force.

Prithā Arjuna's mother (also called Kuntī). Arjuna is called Pārtha, "son of Prithā."

Purusha ["person"] The soul; the spiritual core of every person. In the Gītā, the terms *Ātman* and *Purusha* are virtually interchangeable.

Purushottama "Highest Person," Supreme Being, God.

rāja yoga "The Royal Path"; the path of meditation taught especially by Patanjali in the *Yoga Sūtras*.

rajas See under *guna*.

Rāma "Prince of Joy," name of the son of Dasharatha, who was king of Ayodhyā. Rāma was the famous prince who killed the evil demon Rāvana to reclaim his wife Sītā. He is regarded as an incarnation of Vishnu.

Rig Veda The oldest of the four Vedas, the most ancient and sacred Hindu scriptures.

Rudras A group of gods associated with storm and destruction. Sometimes the Rudras are mentioned as a group; at other times they are thought of as a single god, Rudra. In later Hinduism, Shiva is called Rudra.

sādhana A body of disciplines or way of life which leads to the supreme goal of Self-realization.

sādhu A holy man, sage.

Sahadeva One of the junior Pāndava brothers.

Sāma Veda The Veda of songs and chants. One of the four Vedas.

samādhi Mystical union with God; a state of intense concentration in which consciousness is completely unified.

samsāra The world of flux; the round of birth, decay, death and rebirth.

Sanjaya The sage who divinely perceives what is taking place on the battlefield and reports it to the blind king Dhritarāshtra.

Sānkhya One of the six branches of Hindu philosophy. Sānkhya seeks to liberate the individual *Purusha* (spirit) from *prakriti* (mind and matter).

sannyāsa Renunciation.

sat [from *as* "to be"] The Real; truth; goodness.

sattva See under *guna*.

satya Truth, truthful; good, the Good.

savikalpa samādhi [*sa-vikalpa* "having distinctions" or "admitting separateness"] Samādhi in which some duality of subject and object remains, the devotee being absorbed in meditation without becoming completely identified with the object of contemplation; union with the personal God.

Shakti Power; God's feminine aspect; the Divine Mother.

shama Peace; the peace of deep meditation.

Shankara "Giver of peace," a name of Shiva.

Shiva The third person of the Hindu Trinity, the other two being Brahmā, the Creator, and Vishnu, the Preserver. Shiva destroys, but he also conquers death.

shraddhā Faith.

shūdra The fourth Hindu caste; a worker or servant.

Skanda A god of war, the son of Shiva; general of the divine forces when they go into battle against the demons.

soma A drink used in Vedic ritual; the drink of the gods.

Srī [pronounced *shrī*] A title of respect originally meaning "auspicious" or "holy."

svadharma The duty appropriate to a particular person, one's own individual dharma.

tamas See under *guna*.

tapas Austerity, control of the senses; the spiritual power acquired through self-control.

tyāga Renunciation.

Upanishads Ancient mystical documents found at the end of each of the four Vedas.

Ushanas A sage and poet who appears in the Vedas.

varna Caste or class.

Varuna God of waters and the ocean; in the Vedas, the moral overseer of the world.

Vāsuki The king of the serpents, he lives in the underworld and balances the earth on his serpent hood.

Veda [from *vid* "to know"] "Knowledge"; the name of the most ancient Sanskrit scriptures, considered to be a direct revelation from God to the mystics of the past.

vidyā Knowledge, wisdom; a science or branch of study.

vijnāna Knowledge, judgment, understanding.

Vishnu Second in the Hindu Trinity; the Preserver who incarnates himself in age after age for the establishment of dharma and for the welfare of all creatures.

Vivasvat The sun god, the father of Manu, the ancestor of mankind.

Vrishni Name of an important clan of ancient north India. According to legend the Vrishnis all perished at the end of Krishna's life when their city, Dvāraka, sank in the sea.

Vyāsa The sage revered as the author of the *Mahābhārata* and the Gītā. He was the father of both Dhritarāshtra and Pāndu, and he gave Sanjaya the power of mystic vision so that he could behold the dialogue between Srī Krishna and Arjuna.

yajna Offering, sacrifice, worship.

Yajur One of the four Vedas.

yoga [from *yuj* "to unite"] Union with God, realization of the unity of all life; a path or discipline which leads to such a state of total integration or unity. Yoga is also the name of one of the six branches of Hindu philosophy, and as such is paired with Sānkhya.

yogī A person who practices spiritual disciplines.

Yudhishthira Arjuna's elder brother, famous for his adherence to dharma at all times.

yuga An age or eon. In Hindu cosmology there are four yugas, representing a steady deterioration in the state of the world from age to age. The names of the yugas are taken from

a game of dice. Krita Yuga is the age of perfection, followed by Tretā Yuga. The incarnation of Srī Krishna is said
to mark the end of the third yuga, Dvāpara. We are living
in the fourth and final yuga, Kali, in which the creation
reaches its lowest point. The world goes through 1,000 such
yuga-cycles during one kalpa or Day of Brahma.

॥ *Index*

action, *see* selfless action
adharma, 267
advaita, 26
Agni, 23
ahamkara, 39, 211, 223
ahimsa, 32
ajnana, 147
akasha, 214
Ananta, 181
anger, 87, 102, 103, 126, 221
Aquinas, St. Thomas, 18, 37
Arjuna: background, 15; becomes
    seeker after truth, 179; concern
    over how to act, 99; doubting heart,
    114–15; family tragedy, 72, 111; and
    Krishna, 15, 19, 21–22, 71–72, 84, 171,
    191–93; as man of action, 21, 83, 102;
    portrayal in Bhagavad Gita, 71–72;
    real Self, 83–84
Aryan tribes, 16, 23
asat, 245
ashrams, 17
ashvattha, 229
Ashvatthama, 74
asuras, 181, 237
Atman: at climax of meditation, 26;
    defined, 24; Krishna as, 180, 229;
    play on word, 135; relationship
    to Brahman, 26; as Self, 30;
    transcended by Krishna, 229; in
    Upanishads, 24, 203; *see also* Self
attachment, 54–55, 61, 87, 101, 114, 123,
    153

Augustine, St., 18, 37, 60
avatara, 112
avyakta, 164
avyayam padam, 230

Bede, St., 7
Bhagavad Gita: about, 9–10, 14, 113;
    as an Upanishad, 18–19; as book
    of choices, 66; chapter-ending
    formula, 19; contrast with rest of
    Mahabharata, 19–20; essence,
    48–59; heart of message, 20–21;
    and issue of self-mastery, 15, 21; and
    Kurukshetra, 14–15; multiple gods
    in, 23; setting, 15–22; as shruti, 18; as
    spiritual instruction, 21–22; types
    of yoga in, 48–50; way of love in,
    204–6
Bhagavan, 71, 179
bhakti, 171
bhakti yoga, 49
Bhima, 72
Bhishma, 15, 73, 74
Brahma, 149, 163–64
Brahman: about, 24; defined, 24, 213;
    knowledge of, 125; and Om, 245; and
    process of death, 160; relationship
    to Atman, 26; and still mind, 137;
    union with, 254; in Upanishads, 24,
    179, 203–4; and world-tree, 229
brahmarandhra, 160, 161
brahmavidya, 17
Brihadaranyaka Upanishad, 162

Buddha, 123–24, 126, 137, 203, 212
buddhi, 39

castes, 253
Catherine of Genoa, St., 56–57
Catherine of Siena, St., 62
cause and effect, *see* karma
chakras, 160
Chandogya Upanishad, 161
Chesterton, G. K., 60
Christ, 56, 203
Christian mystics, 205; St. Augustine,
    18, 37, 60; St. Catherine of Genoa,
    56–57; St. Francis of Assisi, 51, 60,
    62; St. John of the Cross, 64, 126, 135,
    205; St. Paul, 205; St. Teresa of Avila,
    62, 126, 192
The Cloud of Unknowing, 205
consciousness: as divine ground of
    existence, 213; dreaming as state of,
    28; dreamless sleep as state of, 28;
    human exploration, 8, 10; impact
    of selfless work on, 59; Krishna as,
    181; in meditation, 26; at moment of
    death, 159–61; natural state, 47; and
    Sankhya, 39–41; and self-will, 53; as
    setting for Bhagavad Gita, 21–22;
    and sleep, 28, 35; states of, 28; testing
    levels of awareness, 26; unitary, 47;
    waking as state of, 28; withdrawing
    from hold on senses, 42; *see also*
    mind
cosmology, 44, 164
Cousins, Norman, 63
creation: and Brahman, 229; cycles of
    regeneration and decay, 112, 163; and
    Day of Brahma, 44; and dharma,
    24; indivisible, 32; and Krishna, 112,
    148, 169; and union of prakriti and
    Purusha, 148
cyclical universe, 157, 163–64

Day of Brahma, 44, 163, 164
death: Arjuna's questions, 158; and
    Brahman, 160; consciousness at
    moment of death, 159–61; and
    karma, 163; Krishna's instructions,
    36; and rebirth, 158; role of yogis,

159–60, 161; Upanishad account, 36,
    159–60, 161
dehavat, 204
Desai, Mahadev, 50
desire, 52
detachment, 54–55, 60–61, 84, 85, 114,
    125, 134, 138
devas, 23, 237, 244
devotion, 112, 193, 203–6, 254; *see also*
    bhakti yoga
Dhammapada, 9
dharma, 24, 31–32, 75, 112
dharmakshetra, 67
Dhritarashtra, 72, 73, 255
Dionysius, 204
Donne, John, 32
Drona, 15, 73–74
Duryodhana, 73
dvandva, 181
Dvaraka, 15

Eckhart, Meister, 18, 56, 58, 65, 126
Eddington, Arthur, 25
ego, 26, 36, 39, 52–53, 57, 87
Emerson, Ralph Waldo, 212
evolution, 47, 65

faith, *see* shraddha
field of forces, 25, 35, 37, 43, 46, 212
fields, 211, 212, 213
fig tree, 229
forest academies, 17
Francis of Assisi, St., 51, 60, 62

gambling, 182
Gandhi, Mahatma: and Bhagavad
    Gita, 10, 14, 20, 60, 75, 86; and
    detachment, 54–55; as fully human,
    62; and selfless action, 51
Ganges, 180
gayatri, 181
gunas: defined, 43, 44; as fabric
    of existence, 44–45; and faith,
    243, 244–45; and maya, 150;
    and personality, 46–47; as
    qualities of prakriti, 221–23; and
    Sankhya philosophy, 102–3, 253;
    transcending, 222–23

guru, 74, 84

Hastinapura, 73
hatha yoga, 85, 133
hell, 236
Hinduism: dharma and karma in, 31; multiple gods in, 23; multiplicity of names for aspects of God, 22–23; and path of knowledge, 203; and path of moderation, 136; proclaims one God, 22; Shiva and Shakti in, 213
holy name, *see* mantram
Hume, David, 26
Huxley, Aldous, 17

Indra, 23, 180
Ishvara, 229

Janaka, 103
Jesus Christ, 56, 203
jiva, 84
jnana, 147, 148
jnana yoga, 48, 50, 101–2
John of the Cross, St., 64, 126, 135, 205

kala, 193
kama, 86
Kama Sutra, 136
Kapila, 37
karma: about, 33–34; in Bhagavad Gita, 100–101; and consequences of shraddha, 65; defined, 24; and hell, 236; and process of death, 163; and rebirth, 170; and selfish attachment, 101, 252; in Upanishads, 24
karma phala, 53, 125, 252
karma yoga: and Bhagavad Gita, 49, 50, 51–52; defined, 49; goal of, 114; as selfless action, 99–103, 124–25, 134
Katha Upanishad, 230
Kauravas, 72
Kempis, Thomas à, 62
knower of field, 38, 211, 213, 214, 229
knowledge: of Brahman, 125; as fruit of doing, 114; of Self, 60, 124–25; *see also* jnana yoga
Krishna: and Arjuna, 15, 19, 21–22, 71–72, 84, 171, 191–93; as Atman, 180, 229; in Bhagavad Gita, 19, 149, 169; as Creator, 148–49; deep revelation of his divine being, 179–82; divine nature, 112–13, 191–93; exalted nature, 169–72, 230; home of, 164, 230–31; as Lord, 21; as name for aspect of God, 23; need for devotion to, 171–72; and prakriti and Purusha, 148–49; as prana of body, 231; and rebirth, 111–12; remembering at hour of death, 158–59; and renunciation, 55–56; reveals divine powers and attributes, 179–82; role in Bhagavad Gita, 15, 19, 71–72; royal secret, 172; as Self, 22, 58, 180, 181, 229; transcends Atman, 229; "two natures" of, 148; as Vishnu, 192; and yoga in Bhagavad Gita, 49, 50
kundalini, 136
Kuru dynasty, 13, 71, 72–73
Kurukshetra, 13, 14–15

lila, 149
lotus, 125, 149
love: of God, 204–6; selfless, 170

madbhavam, 158
Madhusudana, 237
Mahabharata: basis in actual events, 15; defined, 13; and human good and evil, 237; Krishna in, 113; and Kurukshetra, 13, 14–15; as metaphor, 21; and morality of war, 75; relationship of Bhagavad Gita to, 14, 18–20
Mallory, George Leigh, 8
manas, 39
mantram: Krishna as, 181; Om as, 161, 181, 245; Om Tat Sat as, 245
maya: about, 28–30; in Bhagavad Gita, 150; defined, 28, 150; and Krishna, 112, 150; in Rig Veda, 151; in Sankhya philosophy, 150; in Vedanta, 150; and wheel of time, 254
meditation: consciousness in, 26; evidence in Indus Valley, 16; final stage, 26, 192; finding place for,

135–36; and one-pointed mind, 135, 136; reasons for doing, 134, 205; as samadhi, 125–26; unity within, 26; and yoga, 134; *see also* raja yoga

Meera, 126

mind: and change, 25; comparing to flame, 137; as field of forces, 25, 37, 43, 46, 212; in final stage of meditation, 26, 192; at hour of death, 158–59, 160; impact of selflessness on, 53, 59; levels of awareness, 26; making one-pointed, 135, 136; and material elements, 41; and renunciation, 51; role in directing the soul toward rebirth, 158; and Sankhya, 37, 39–40; still, 47–48; training, 87, 137–38; *see also* consciousness

moha, 150–51

Mohammed, 56, 203

moksha, 24, 30, 126, 252

morality of war, 74–75

Moses, 56, 134

Muhammad, *see* Mohammed

mukta, 126

Nakula, 72

nirvana, 30, 52

nirvikalpa samadhi, 192

nishkama karma, 52, 53

offerings, 114, 171; *see also* yajna

Om (mantram), 161, 181, 245

Om Tat Sat (mantram), 245

Oppenheimer, Robert, 193

pada, 230

Pandavas, 72, 73

Patanjali, 133, 159, 192

Paul, St., 205

Perennial Philosophy, 17, 18, 22

physics, 24–25, 29, 37, 44, 164

pipal trees, 229

Prahlada, 181

prakriti: about, 37, 43–44, 56; aspects of, 212; components of, 211; as field, 212, 213; and gunas, 43, 221–23; and

karma, 212; nature of, 221–23; in Sankhya philosophy, 148; union with Purusha, 148

pranas, 160–61, 231

Purusha: defined, 37, 38; as knower, 213; liberation from gunas, 222–23; in Sankhya philosophy, 148; Shiva as, 214; union with prakriti, 148; in Upanishads, 151

Purushottama, 179

raja yoga, 49, 134; *see also* meditation

rajas: defined, 44, 45; as one of three gunas, 44, 46, 102, 103, 243, 244–45; as quality of prakriti, 221, 222; transforming tamas into, 47; and work, 253

rakshasas, 244

Rama, 181, 237

Ramakrishna, 126, 147–48

Ramana Maharshi, 126

Ramayana, 181

Ravana, 237

realization, *see* Self-realization; vijnana

rebirth, 84, 111–12, 170

reincarnation, 35; *see also* rebirth

renunciation: and Bhagavad Gita, 51, 53–54; defined, 58; as essence of Bhagavad Gita, 51; and gunas, 252; as path to real peace of mind, 206; sannyasa type *vs.* tyaga type, 251–52

Rig Veda, 16, 22, 151, 181, 230

rishis, 17, 24

Rudra, 181

Ruysbroeck, Jan van, 27, 29, 57

sada, 126

sadhana, 244

sadhu, 136, 172, 212

Sahadeva, 72

samabuddhi, 135

samadhi: Arjuna's, 191–93; defined, 30; at moment of death, 161; nirvikalpa, 192; potter's wheel analogy, 59; savikalpa, 192; as state of profound meditation, 125–26, 179

samsara, 24, 35, 84, 86

Sanjaya, 74, 255

Sankhya philosophy: about, 37–38; categories of gunas in, 102–3, 253; defined, 37; and mango analogy, 40; mind and matter, 38–43; prakriti and Purusha in, 37–38, 148; *vs.* yoga, 37, 124

sannyasa, 123, 124, 251; *see also* renunciation

Sanskrit language, 16

sat, 245

sattva: defined, 44, 45; harnessing energy of rajas into, 47; as one of three gunas, 44, 46, 102, 243, 244; as quality of prakriti, 221, 222; and spiritual disciplines, 244; and work, 253

savikalpa samadhi, 192

Self: Atman as, 30; at climax of meditation, 26, 48; at conception, 231; and gunas, 46; and Krishna, 22, 58, 180, 181, 229; relationship to action, 56, 113; *see also* Atman

self-discipline, 135, 244

Self-knowledge, 60, 125

Self-realization, 58–59, 83–87, 134

self-will, 52–53

selfishness, 51, 102; *see also* renunciation

selfless action, 51–52, 53, 99, 124–25; *see also* karma yoga

selfless love (bhakti), 170

selfless service, 57–58, 99–103, 114, 124, 244

senses: as "gates" of body, 160; and sense objects, 41–43; training, 87

Sermon on the Mount, 14, 20, 60

Shakti, 213–14

shama, 134

Shankara, 18, 37, 59, 126, 181

Shaw, Bernard, 62

Shiva, 16, 22, 181, 213, 214

shraddha, 63–65, 243–44

shruti, 18

siddhi, 253–54

soul, *see* jiva

sudurachara, 172

tamas: defined, 44, 45; as one of three gunas, 44, 46, 102, 103, 243, 244, 245; as quality of prakriti, 221–22; transforming into rajas, 47; and work, 253

tanha, 52

tanmatras, 41

tapas, 244–45

Tat, 230, 245

tattvas, 38–43

Teresa of Avila, St., 62, 126, 192

Troy, 15

turiya, 28, 29–30

tyaga, 206, 251–52

unity: in climax of meditation, 26; discovering, 42; glimpsing, 126; as goal of evolution, 47; as multiplicity, 29–30; as state of consciousness, 28; unitive state, 27, 28

universe, cyclical, 157, 163–64

Upanishads: about, 8–9, 23–24; account of death process, 36, 159–60, 161; as background for Bhagavad Gita, 22–36; discoveries of brahmavidya in, 17–18; as minimum sources of Hinduism, 18; and Perennial Philosophy, 18; and pranas, 231; Purusha in, 151; states of consciousness in, 28; in Vedas, 18; *vs.* Bhagavad Gita, 22, 203–4

Varuna, 23, 181

Vasudeva, 182

Vedanta, 150

Vedas, 18, 169–70, 181, 203, 230

vibhutis, 179, 182

vijnana, 147, 148, 150

Vishnu: as Creator, 149; defined, 112; Krishna as, 71, 112, 113, 180, 192; measuring cosmos, 230; role of Brahma in, 149; Shiva and Shakti, 214

Vrishni, 182

Vyasa, 19, 21, 74, 182, 255

wheel of time, 254

wisdom, *see* jnana; vijnana

work, *see* selfless action
world-tree, 229
worship, *see* yajna

Yadavas, 71
yajna, 57, 114
yoga: and Bhagavad Gita, 22, 48–49; bhakti, 49; central principle, 47; common meaning, 51; defined, 30, 85, 134; jnana, 48, 50, 101–2; karma, 49, 50, 51–52, 99–103, 114, 124–25, 134; raja, 49, 134; significance of word, 56; *vs.* Sankhya, 124
Yoga, as school of meditation, 37
Yoga, Lord of, 16, 193
yoga psychology, 37–48
Yoga Sutras, 133, 159, 192
Yogeshvara, 16
yogis: in Bhagavad Gita, 133–35; defined, 134; role in process of death, 159–60, 161; true, 135
Yudhishthira, 72, 73
yugas, 164

Blue Mountain Center of Meditation

The Blue Mountain Center of Meditation publishes Eknath Easwaran's books, videos, and audio recordings, and offers retreats and online programs on his eight-point program of passage meditation.

For more information and resources, please visit:
www.bmcm.org

The Blue Mountain Center of Meditation
Box 256, Tomales, California 94971 USA

Telephone: +1 707 878 2369
Toll-free in the US: 800 475 2369
Email: info@bmcm.org

EKNATH EASWARAN (1910–1999) brings to this volume a rare combination of credentials: knowledge of Sanskrit, an intuitive understanding of his Hindu legacy, and a mastery of English. He was chairman of the English department at a major Indian university when he came to

the United States on a Fulbright fellowship in 1959.

A gifted teacher who lived for many years in the West, Easwaran explains the concepts underlying the classics of Indian spirituality in fresh, authoritative, and profoundly simple ways.